Secrets of
The Shangri-La
Warrior
The Shambala Guide to Success

Mysticism Buddhism Gnosticism Zen Taoism Shinto Hindu Zoroaster Sumerian
Spirituality Shamanism Ancient Religion Metaphysics Ethics and Philosophy

Sgr. George Mentz, JD, MBA, CWM, DSS, International Lawyer & Sgr. De Blondel
Written by a former top wealth advisor of a Wall Street firm

The Greatest Success Secrets Ever Known!

Shangri La – Guide to Prosperity, Peace and Success

~ Many are Called but Few are Chosen

IN TIBETAN BUDDHIST AND INDIAN TRADITIONS, SHAMBHALA IS A MYTHICAL KINGDOM HIDDEN SOMEWHERE IN INNER ASIA

MAGUS INCOGNITO

Secrets of Shangri La - Contents

This May be The Greatest Self-Help Guide Ever Written

If you have read all of the books on self-help, human potential and spirituality, then this one will bring it all together. This is the magnum opus of all success books. This short book is a compilation of the most important keys to warrior success and covers the major topics of success, harmony, abundance and wealth that the greatest philosophers and gurus have discovered.

1. The guide covers the secret powers of the Shangri La Warrior and the missing code to grow rich and how to develop habits for peace, prosperity and success. You will love this short book if f you have enjoyed books by the great success gurus such as: Buddha, Marcus Aurelius, Confucius, Pythagoras, Laozi – Lao Tzu, Confucius Born, Siddhartha Gautama Buddhism, or other great teachers, then this book may provide the clarity and illumination that you are seeking.

2.

We have taken thousands of pages of information and condensed it into this powerful guide. Rarely have we seen a person fail who has used these timeless and proven techniques.

This book can create that shift and awakening that you have been waiting to achieve for years. Keep this booklet close, study it and become a master of your destiny.

The Great Teachers and YOU

This book is a summary of some of the greatest teachings about peace and prosperity throughout history. Herein, we will be addressing some of the best success ideas from greatest cultures of all time. To begin with, all of the great masters have suggested that *you are what you think*, that mastery is a result of your overall thinking and, generally speaking, that your well-being is a result of your spiritual-mental condition. The major prosperity thinkers and gurus of metaphysics will say that each of us has the right to make the best of ourselves. It's a natural law. It's a human right that we should all be able to maximize our lives and to exercise our individual talents to our highest abilities.

This book is for those who desire wealth and prosperity. The wisdom herein is for seekers who are open to new perspectives and who want to live to the fullest. This manuscript is designed to help readers make a difference in the world by helping people make the best of themselves and their opportunities. For those of you who want more out of life, and who are tired of failure, this collection of timeless success wisdom will show you the path to achievement and the keys to prosperity. Do not sit idly by and reject or deny the abundance of the world—abundance awaits your cooperation and inquiry.

The world is plentiful with resources, and your creativity is one of the many secrets to your future success. You do not need money to plan and to begin working on an idea; you do not need a special talent or to save every penny to be rich. You do not need the perfect business location for your offices. Many people become rich with no talent, no college education, a less than perfect place to work and live, and no start-up capital. The time is now to change your mind about life and to begin anew. When you are ready and willing to improve your life and to open your heart and mind, the gold mine of abundance will be available to you. The whole world of past and present is looking toward you, waiting for you to achieve your dreams; all you need to do is make the mental and spiritual shift in consciousness.

Much of this book is about tapping into the energy of the universe. Many call it spiritual or cosmic energy, or God force or power. There are various words that have been used over the centuries to describe the Source and obtaining flow and unity with universal power—God, Spirit, the Good, Universal Mind, Deity, Lord, Infinite, Almighty, Creator, and Universal Life Force. In this book, I will focus on Abundance, or the everlasting creative forces or powers that are available to anyone who wants to be an architect of good and constructive things in order to better one's own life and the lives of those one cares about in this world.

Chapter 1 - The Inner Power of You – Becoming a Superstar

As some point, all of us develop an internal hunger for a higher purpose and to master our destiny during our lives. This instinctive fire in the belly seemingly compels us to think and take action; we must change and adapt. Growth is necessary for the human condition. Finding a reason for being, where we can cultivate our talents and use them to improve life for ourselves and those we love, becomes vitally important. Striving for the personal best in ourselves while serving humanity is an ideal both important and noble. It is part of our desire for a greater good. Becoming the best we can be and doing the things we love to do in service and in leisure is a natural desire. This is true whether one is a righteous member if any religion or a follower of a philosophical practices, virtues, and ethics.   The state of Abundance is possible when we inherently understand the need to adapt, grow, and be prepared. You hold the golden key when you master your destiny by improving yourself in mind body and spirit.

This codex is a summary of the key philosophy and secrets needed to advance to your highest potential. If you need to learn even more to prepare yourself for this guide, we suggest several other authors: Marcus Aurelius, the gospels of Jesus Christ, Buddha, Pythagoras, Hegel, Kant, Emerson, von Goethe, Meister Eckhart, poetic Vedas and Eddas, The Book of Psalms, Zoroaster, Lao Tzu, Socrates, Plato, Aristotle, the Upanishads, and any great wisdom literature. Then, of course, readers are encouraged to seek more light from the authors in the bibliography.

One of the greatest secrets of mankind is that leaders and professionals have quietly used the philosophy contained herein for centuries. Keep this book close, use this secret technology, and master your destiny.

Whatever our vocation may be (e.g., mechanic or artist), you will need the right instruction and tools to gain excellence. The importance of natural expression is absolutely necessary for personal accomplishment and prosperity. Your highest form of expression requires an imaginative and resourceful life; it involves the abundance of ideas, things, and actions.

True and lasting prosperity has a spiritual foundation and balance. Genuine success is mastering excellence in body, mind, and spirit. When there is balance, ideas and energy naturally come from the universe to the person who is exercising this higher order of existence. When we are at our best and acting as effective individuals, we actually have more insights flowing to us from the universal source or consciousness of the infinite.

Now let us focus firstly on the great philosophers of science and ethics. These great thinkers all contribute different ingredients to the recipe of a rich and fuller life. Read what each of them has to say, ponder their ideas, and then you will be ready to examine the rest of the book.

- Rene Descartes simplifies the essence of philosophy: "I think, therefore I am." With this statement, we must be able to find our being, or what people call their being-ness. The key is to reconnect your spirit and deeper-self with the universe in a way that is harmonious.

- George W. F. Hegel, a German philosopher, also believed that reality was absolute Spirit; we participate in our destinies and create our own realities.

- Meister Eckhart, the fourteenth-century Christian Neo-Platonist, personified the spiritual basics in these words: "If the only prayer you say in your life is 'Thank You,' that would suffice."

- Socrates said, "Know thyself," and, "The unexamined life is not worth living." Be willing to take a hard look at yourself in the mirror, and seek an honest appraisal of your character and behavior and seek greater heights.

- The French existentialist Jean-Paul Sartre was clear about accountability. We should start having responsibility for our actions going forward and refuse to be bogged down with self-victimization and blame.

- Ben Franklin, in his autobiography, used a process called the precept of order, where each day he took time to review his day, set goals, and see where he could improve his actions and character.

- Nietzsche said, "That which does not kill us makes us stronger," Thus, we need to face fear and rise above our comfort zones.

- Marcus Aurelius so eloquently said, "Take full account of the excellencies which you possess, and in gratitude remember how you would hanker after them, if you had them not." Aurelius stated another great quote that we should follow: "It is not death that a man should fear, but he should fear never beginning to live."

- Humanistic psychologists Carl Rogers and Abraham Maslow believed that people have an innate drive to be all they can be and to self-actualize. This intrinsic metaphysics plays a large role in facilitating the progression of the best in each of us.

- Aristotle formulated a theory of potentiality: "Within each of us is a natural evolution toward fulfilling our potential."

- Immanuel Kant has implied that OUR Perception IS our reality. If you focus your thoughts on the best, then you will attract the best. Feed yourself with things that are good, learning about what is excellent, and these things will build your worldview and character.

- Dr. Carl Jung theorized that one finds their natural talents deep within the spirit of one's self. When we get in touch with our natural inclinations, it elevates our outward expression. It may not be easy, but if you act toward your higher purpose each day, the cosmic momentum will build to your advantage.

- Both Aristotle and Thomas Aquinas refer to God as the 'First Cause" or "Pure Mind." In essence, we come from this pure mind and first cause; we are created from the Source. We have desires and ideas flowing to us from a higher source at all times. What you do with your ideas and imagination is of extreme importance. Your ideas are yours, they are priceless, and they are consciously coming to you in every moment. Your creativity is your abundance.

- The poet Johann Wolfgang von Goethe famously stated that "Boldness is genius."

- Acclaimed self help author Robert Collier also believed that beginning any task created a nucleus of activity, bringing form from the formless. If you begin something and maintain faith in the process, you may then utilize the act of gratitude and praise which is like watering a flower with nourishment. In the same way a flower needs water, the universe craves peace, thanks, praise, and action, and the universe will respond accordingly with blessings.

- Engels and Marx believed firmly in productivity as the key to progress. The big metaphysical secret lies in becoming one with your desires, because you then become in tune with your objective! When we blend purpose and spirituality, our energy then becomes laser focused.

- The philosopher of existentialism Soren Kierkegaard was famous for saying, "We must think for ourselves and be suspicious of groupthink, and we should not worry about the ignorance of neighbors and society."

- Remember, Emerson, St. Augustine, and Plato believed that evil is not a diabolical force but rather the absence of good.

- Henry David Thoreau believed that we should put our "Conscience before conformity." Thus, your natural creativity and labor will be fun, and you will learn to freely accept premiums and rewards for your quality services and the products in relation to your craft.

- British political philosopher John Locke believed in a liberal, anti-authoritarian theory of the state. His practical theory of knowledge advocated religious toleration and personal identity. His philosophy suggests that order is necessary to protect the individual, and man is endowed with inalienable rights where these rights are gained through work and effort.

- Alfred Wallace, the founder of evolution theory with Darwin, systematically came to believe evolution was sometimes guided by a higher power and that evolution could not account for human consciousness.

- The nineteenth-century European philosopher Arthur Schopenhauer believed that we are motivated by our will, and it is our will that is our sense of reality. Therefore, willingness is at the core of our growth and advancement. Desire is good and comes from the Spirit. Seeing past the illusion of what seems apparent, and acting on healthy desires, is the key to growth and happiness.

Whether you are a student of Locke, Emerson, Ayn Rand, Ben Franklin, Frederick Douglas, or Buddha, we all benefit from these eternal truths. The great lesson from many of the world's legendary philosophers is that the individual is an important and unique part of the whole. Each person should master themselves; education, knowledge, and inner peace are essential. Efficient effort is vital for advancement. Growing in faith, knowingness, and wisdom are all important factors of our duty to ourselves and to society. Your contributions may seem small, but your spiritual creativity and service may positively affect generations to come. Overall, the ripple effect of one pebble tossed in the lake has a broad impact on the whole of its contents. Thus our individual betterment benefits all.

The outcome of practicing these principles and suggestions will result in a natural expression of your life's true purpose that becomes a reality—you will become who you were meant to be. It may require a real commitment from you, but it will eventually feel like child's play. You may find many challenges, but the experience of life will be invigorating when you pause in those moments to stop and smell the roses. Life is delicate and sometimes short, and you may be compelled to dedicate energy to definitive ends. All mortals are faced with these timeless questions: What do you want to be remembered for? How do you want to impact the world? What is your potential legacy?

The great masters have many similar teachings about spiritual matters, but the insights sound the same. The masters declare that " You have within you the power to connect to the universal force. This force is the creative and animating energy that permeates the universe. Like gravity or electricity, the Power is not seen, but exists as the all-pervading framework for which every law hinges upon. This all pervading force is also known as God or "The Life Force". This unlimited power is everywhere as creation is constant. New ideas, new art & music, new planets, new galaxies, new species, new worlds are continuously manifesting at this very moment in tandem with this Power. The unique part of your mind that can be in-tune with this force is referred to by the great teachers of metaphysics as the subjective mind or higher consciousness.

Directed thought-energy can be focused where the individual may act as a creative force within the universal framework. This supernatural power is willing to serve you and grant you anything constructive that you earnestly and sincerely desire with focus, action, heartfelt gratitude and emotion.

If Faith is the substance of things hoped for, then that very Substance can also be qualified as the energy of our attention and thoughts. Belief and faith are the same in that they mean that we accept what is unseen. Energy is consciousness, and thus, "thought awareness" is energy. All things created equally in perfect balance, the energy of faith, attention, and mind can tilt the cosmic balance of life, happiness, and success in our favor.

All of us go through life with a steady stream of ideas, thoughts, and desires. Tapping into that greater, infinite-self expands our intuitive abilities to best use our priceless inspiration. Thus, becoming aware that we may operate at a higher order of being is where achievement truly begins, and then, we become willing to take the actions that provide results. Co-operation with the "force of the universe" and the framework of the metaphysical laws that affect mankind is the path to maximize our existence, contributions, and consciousness.

From Taoism to Christianity, and from Eastern and Western cultures, the mystics believed in a timeless and formless force that governs the cosmos. Most of the founding fathers of the United

States were deists who believed in the Source or a supreme God. We are born of this cosmic force, and we have the ability to more effectively cooperate as spiritual and physical beings in conjunction with this force. Listen to your heart and allow yourself to become and evolve into your highest expression; get in tune with the world and allow yourself to manifest your Quantum Bliss....

DESIRE AND PURPOSE

Desire is the motivating force that rules the world. Even with today's attitudes where science, philosophy, and religious metaphysics cross paths, most have acknowledge that finding: purpose, natural expression, mission, and finding your true place are all major factors in self-expression and spirit-manifestation. Where a person's true purpose is frustrated, reactions take place and most people are guided and again re-directed by their burning desires toward their highest ideal of creativity and function.

ATTRACTION, SOWING, REAPING, KARMA AND THE LAW OF CORRESPONDENCES

Overall, it has been said, repeated thoughts become tendencies or habits, willingness can become action, and repeated experiences lead to wisdom. Our thoughts, actions, inactions and omissions are what create our character.

If we desire harmonious & peaceful energy, we must be willing to put out good thoughts, praise others, become thankful, see things in an opportunistic light, have faith in the regeneration of mind and body and take right actions. Our every action and thought of goodness is very powerful. Acts of kindness, service to others and self-development are all extremely powerful energies. Negative feelings are feeble thoughts, which are a hundred times less powerful than acts of creation and constructiveness. If we maintain a harmonious relationship with the Supreme Intelligence while keeping a peaceful relationship with our externals, life will of course, be much easier. Further, when we are avoiding wasteful thinking and actions, our spiritual energies maintain a laser focus and power. As with Physics, it is possible to neutralize a sound wave by setting up another sound wave of the same pattern which comes from the opposite pole. Therefore, it is possible to conjure and visualize ideas, thoughts, and images that can completely neutralize old attitudes. By changing your outlook, you can change your future. Every cause has its effect and every action has its results, but it is desire that is the link that connects the two.

You may feel you have wronged many people. You may even feel guilty for past deeds or encounters. However, if you feel remorse and intend to act as a better person for now on, then you have made progress. In any event, your day-to-day action and character of goodness and kindness will build your positive energy where the world will protect you and serve you.

ATONEMENT AND PURITY OF MIND

Steps to the Mastery of Attunement – The clearing away mental debris through a process of self analysis and attunement will allow us to learn what we want from life and what we do not want.

1.   Maintain Humility - remain teachable, and being right-sized with regard to ego.

2.   Developing Character - Seek change and growth in your favor.

3.   Honesty and Integrity - Do what you say and be honest with yourself.

4.   Purity of Thought, Heart, and Intentions – Keep your thinking clear, act now, and enjoy the moment.

5.   Selflessness - Giving without expectation of return through service and non-hoarding of things and yourself. Circulate your goodness and radiate your excellence.

6.   Develop Higher Purpose - Making healthy decisions to become definite toward your objectives or advancement for all.

7.   Gratitude—Be thankful for the gifts you have received, praising others, blessing your home, family, and world.

8.   Reflection – Maintain willingness to engage self-analysis and evaluation for the purposes of growth.

9.   Attunement - Seek harmony with others through amends, restitution, mental catharsis, character development, and right action.

10.   Visualization - Use of contemplation, prayer, or meditation to enable a mental vision of a fuller life and connection to the Universe.

11.   Open Mind – Keep a motivation to be open-minded about accepting a state of well-being and peace of mind.

12.   Harmony – Allow peace and tranquility in your life and embrace a sincere belief that life is abundant.

PHILOSOPHY OF ABUNDANCE USING GRATITUDE

First, there is the force of creation from which all things proceed. Second, this force gives you everything you desire, and third, you relate yourself to it by a feeling of deep and profound gratitude. Further, the world is overflowing with good things, because life is in touch with the limitless source of all good things, and there is so much of everything that the earnest hunger of every heart can be gratified. We do not have to take from anyone to have abundance, because there is more than sufficient for all. The fact that someone has abundance does not prove that he has taken some or all of his wealth from others, although this is what a great many believe to be the truth. The Universe is overflowing with abundance. If we have not everything that we want, there is a reason. There may be some definite cause somewhere, either in ourselves or in our relations to the world, and when this cause can be found and corrected; then we may proceed to take possession of advancement.

Multitudes continue in poverty from no other cause than a lack of gratitude. If it is a new thought that gratitude brings your whole being into closer harmony with the creative energies of the Universe, consider it well, and you will see that it is true. In the past, we have not stayed true to abundance. Having received one gift from God, people cut the wires that connect them to prosperity by failing to make acknowledgment.

Accordingly, the grateful outreaching of your mind in thankful praise to the supreme intelligence is a liberation or expenditure of force. It cannot fail to reach that to which it addresses, and the reaction is an instantaneous movement toward you. We are now beginning to realize more and more that the greatest thing in the world is to live so closely in-tune with the Infinite that we constantly feel the power and the peace of THE presence. But the value of gratitude does not consist solely in getting you more blessings in the future. Without gratitude you cannot long keep from harboring dissatisfied thoughts regarding things as they are. We also realize that the more closely we live to the Infinite the more we shall receive of all good things, because all good things have their source in the Supreme; but how to enter into this life of supreme oneness with the Most High is the quest of many seekers.

The soul that is always grateful lives nearer the true, the good, the beautiful and the perfect than anyone else in existence. The more closely we live to the good and the beautiful the more we shall receive of all those things.

The grateful mind is constantly fixed upon the best. Therefore it tends to become the best. It takes the form or character of the best, and will receive the best. Also, faith is born of gratitude. The grateful mind continually expects good things, and expectation becomes faith. The reaction of gratitude upon one's own mind produces faith, and every outgoing wave of grateful thanksgiving increases faith.

Notice the grateful attitude that Jesus took, how he always seems to be saying, "I thank thee, Father, that thou hearest me." You cannot exercise much power without gratitude, for it is gratitude that keeps you connected with power. The more grateful we are for the good things that come to us now the more good things we shall receive in the future. This is a great metaphysical law, and we shall find it most profitable to comply exactly with this law, no matter what the circumstances may be.

Be grateful for everything and you will constantly receive more of everything; thus, the simple act of being grateful becomes a path to perpetual increase. The reason is that the mental attitude of authentic gratitude will draw you into much closer contact with that power that produces all excellent and good things received.

In other words, to be grateful for what we have received is to draw more closely to the source of that which we receive. The good things that come to us come because we have properly employed certain laws, and when we are grateful for the results gained, we enter into more perfect harmony with those laws and thus become able to employ those laws to still greater advantage in the immediate future. This anyone can understand, and those who do not know that gratitude produces this effect should try it and watch the results.

The attitude of gratitude brings the whole mind into more perfect and more harmonious relations with all the laws and powers of life. The grateful mind gains a firmer hold, so to speak, upon those things in life that can produce increase. This is simply illustrated in personal experience where we find that we always feel nearer to that person to whom we express real gratitude. When you thank a person and truly mean it with heart and soul you feel nearer to that person than you ever did before. Likewise, when we express our whole-soul in thanksgiving to everything and everybody that comes into our life we draw closer and closer to all the elements and powers of life.

The moment you permit your mind to dwell with dissatisfaction upon things as they are, you begin to lose ground. IF you fix attention upon the common, the ordinary, the poor, the squalid, and the mean, then, your mind may take away your power where you become distracted. Therefore, the person who has no feeling of gratitude cannot long retain a living faith. In other words, to maintain faith, we draw closer to the real source from which all good things in life proceed.

When we consider this principle from another point of view we find the act of being grateful is an absolute necessity, if we wish to accomplish as much as we have the power to accomplish. To be grateful in this large, universal sense is to enter into harmony and contact with the highest and the best in life. We thus gain possession of the superior elements of mind and soul. Consequently, we gain the power to become more and achieve more, no matter what our object or work may be. All of this will place us in a more perfect relation with life, and enable us to appropriate the greater richness of life.

What is gratitude? To be grateful is to think of the best, therefore the grateful mind keeps the eye constantly upon the best. According to another metaphysical law, we grow into the likeness of that which we think of the most. The grateful mind is constantly looking for the best, thus holding attention upon the best and daily growing into the likeness of the best.

The grateful mind expects only good things, and will always secure good things out of everything that comes. What we constantly expect, we can be open to receive. When we constantly expect to acquire good out of everything, then, we cause everything to manifest good toward us. Therefore, to the grateful mind, all things will at all times work together for good, and this means perpetual increase in everything that can add to the happiness and the welfare of man. This being true, and anyone can prove it to be true, the proper course to pursue is to cultivate the habit of being grateful for everything that comes. Give thanks eternally to the Most High for everything and feel deeply grateful every moment to every living creature.

All things are so situated that they can be of some service to us, and all things at some point have been instrumental in adding to our welfare. We must therefore, to be just and true, express continuous gratitude to everything that has existence. Be thankful to yourself and be thankful to every soul in the world, and most importantly, be thankful to the Creator of all that is. Live in perpetual thanksgiving to the entire world, and express the deepest, sincerest, soul-felt gratitude you can feel within whenever something of value comes into your life. When other vacant things come by, we are able to pass them through and never mind them in the least.

ABUNDANCE EVERY DAY - REINVENTION AND REBIRTH

Many people may debate what happens to the soul after the death of the body. To put this discussion in a format we all can understand, let us imagine each day is a new birth and a new opportunity to live again and do the right thing while living under your highest ideals. Each night, our past-self can be allowed to die out and re-incarnate upon the following morning, and we can be born anew. All men and women have the opportunity to: change, atone, grow, regenerate, be reborn and re-awakened. Reincarnation is the great opportunity of man to start to build where construction has ceased. After a death of the ego-self which can happen at any moment, the soul can be malleable and in flux. Some call it openness or a "moment of clarity." At these times, we may be in this rebirthing & transformational stage much as the caterpillar in the cocoon. Dynamic changes and growth can occur rapidly from this state. Thus, our character and spirit can again act rapidly through the laws of desire, purpose, vibration, and attraction.

Then what is the true lesson of Reincarnation? Is it necessary for us to surrender and cooperate in order to be given another opportunity to build the ideal which is our higher order of being? This awakening can occur by virtue of a shift of consciousness, a sacramental initiation, a molecular regeneration, a release of negative thinking by private confession, a confirmation of your path, or a rebirth of the spirit.

Reincarnation for the student of the Soul is the transmuting of the baser desires, the baser ideals, and the base metal, into that fine and pure ideal, and toward a conscious, loving and peaceful existence.

Chapter 2 – The Secrets of Your Destiny

Strategy #1: Metaphysics and Spiritual Economics

The fact remains that *wealth* has been historically viewed as a greedy, godless scramble to capture scarcely allocated resources, but that is just simply not true. There exists unlimited riches in this world, and every time supply of anything runs low, whether it be here or somewhere else, someone creates a substitute for the products or services that had become scarce. In other words, thought-leaders and disruptive genius tends to create new products and services that satisfy the needs and demands of humanity. Are we all creators? The truth of the matter is that *you ARE the totality of your thinking, your actions, and your inactions,* and that your individualized consciousness affects and controls your creative abilities. Thus, you are, in fact, your consciousness which is the essence of your character as a person. A great American metaphysician named Wattles once said, "Every thought or form held in thinking substance causes the creation of the form, but always or at least generally, along the lines of growth an action already established." In general, he is saying that if you impress your thoughts, your creative visualizations, and images clearly in your mind, if you cultivate these thoughts and think about them all day long, if you develop a consciousness of what you want as being accomplished, that form will manifest itself either in you or for you. Another great 20th century teacher, Neville Goddard, has also said, "It is only by a change of consciousness, by actually changing your concept of yourself that you can build more stately mansions, the manifestations of higher and higher concepts." Most of these authors, whether it be Napoleon Hill in the 1920s, Wallace Wattles in 1910, or Charles Haanel in 1910, are saying the same thing: that you must have a burning desire to change, a burning desire to do something, and what that means is you must find a PURPOSE, where you realize what you TRULY want to do and you'd be willing to do anything you can to achieve it.

Strategy #2: Becoming What You Want to BE

And here we come upon the great concept of presumption or the concept of having something in your mind or in your consciousness *before* you actually possess it. Presumption is a wonderful thing because if you presume that you're going to have something and you maintain that "state of faith" each and every day, and you continue taking action to achieve that presumption each day, then it becomes your dominant goal, your primary purpose, and you'll begin to create the snowball effect of focusing the momentum of your mind and your energy towards a particular result. In some cases, you're going to have to let go of your old ideas altogether, and some spiritually minded people would say that you have to let your old-self die-out and let yourself be reborn or reinvented so that you can become who you want to be. And here's the thing: if you want to be something and you're going to eventually *become* that type of person, you're going to need to start acting like "that type of professional". Some say you will be faking it till you make it. If you want to be a Wall Street investment banker, then you're going to have to start playing the part of a Wall Street investment banker. You're going to have to know and understand the rules and the laws and the investment regulations related to being an investment banker. You have to become that person. You will associate with people who are in the business. You have to act the part, and that's what separates mere thinking from being. So the real challenge of the day is that you can learn about the metaphysics, you can do the exercises, you can do the affirmations, but at some point you have to be and act the part, and also you have to know and feel in your heart and in your mind that the results you want belong to you. And the other critical issue is that we need to understand the essence of what we want. The essence is "Why you want something", and if you achieve it, how are you going to use that achievement? How are you going to take advantage of the achievement? How are you going to enjoy the achievement? How will you help improve your world with these advances?

Strategy #3: Affirmations & Contemplation – Boost Your Vibe

As illustrated in many famous books, an affirmation for success is similar to a petition for health using: repeated statements, the present tense, and enthusiasm. What does all this mean?   An affirmation or auto-suggestion should be utilized in a way that invokes feeling and energy at the core of your spirit. This can be called psychological cognitive transformation or PCT. Use prayer, visualization, and affirmations so that your consciousness and vibration is lifted up. If you must hit your knees or gently tap your chest while praying, these techniques can help infuse your spirit with a higher energy and higher connection with the spiritual source of all. Seeing the results of your visualization or affirmation in your mind's eye is part of the visualization process. Feeling what you see in your mind's eye is yet another step.

With the development of our abilities, we learn to picture our goals and dreams in our minds. We further discover how to affirm and cultivate a feeling that "All is right with OUR World." Begin at home and learn to build relationships with complements, praise, and support. Prayer and visualization and feeling are linked on a spiritual and universal level.

In moments of doubtful circumstance, practice gratitude and count your blessings. Affirmations and decrees strengthen your vision and conviction. An affirmation or decree can be a prayer or meditation that asserts our prosperous, happy, and successful bounty. Many people simply say aloud, "I am whole, abundant, complete, healthy, happy, and successful." That is just one example, but you can make up your own positive affirmations. You need not use the words "not" or "no." Affirm by saying, "I am blessed," or "I am happy," or "I am rich in love and life." Whether or not it is your reality at this moment, it should not stand in your way—say it and believe it. Feel it as if it were true right now. The attitude of health, wealth, and peace of mind is a priceless asset that even the richest people on earth cherish.

Examples of Affirmations and Decrees

Prosperity

I am the essence of success. The universe is full of creation and expands every day. New opportunities and new ideas flow to me. I open my heart to that power and participate in the divine ideas that come to me every minute of the day. I allow peace and prosperity in my heart, mind, and soul. I know that I am blessed, and I am thankful for the gift of creation and life expression.

Health

My body is a temple of creation; every organ in my body is nourished and revitalized each day. In time, my whole physical being is regenerated, cell by cell. My mental ideal of myself is perfect. Because I am an offspring of perfect creation, I am made uniquely wonderful through this authority. My body is a vessel of my spirit and soul, which allows me to exist and create in this world. I respect my body and accept the power and opportunity of life, living, and wholeness.

Attitude

My inner spiritual condition allows me to have a high viewpoint of the world. I see the world as a place of kindness, and I become open to receiving the blessings of goodness from others. I see the best in others and myself. I am worthy of success and a wonderful life.

Love

I do all I can to maintain a consciousness of love in my mind. I forgive all those who have passed through my life. I want the best for everyone and aspire to live in harmony, peace, love, and abundance. I meditate on the words of compassion, understanding, peace, humility, kindness, generosity, and selflessness.

Gratitude

I am grateful to all those who have come before me. I am thankful to the supreme creative power for life, peace, health, and the ability to love. Gratitude and a thankful heart keep me connected to power. Gratitude allows me to have faith and the knowledge that I can exist in a higher order of being.

Success

I am successful. I am worthy of prosperity, abundance, health, and happiness. Each day my life becomes better and better.

Health

Here is a Classic Abundant Health Exercise and Meditation in Eight Steps - Read this carefully a few times, and you will come to know the conscious power of healing.   Find a time when you can have 5-10 minutes safe from interruption, and proceed first to make yourself physically comfortable. Lie at ease in a chair, or on a couch, or in bed; it is best to lie flat on your back. If you have no other time, take the exercise on going to bed at night and before rising in the morning.

1) **Relax the Body and Mind:** Let your attention travel over your body from the crown of your head to the soles of your feet, relaxing every muscle as you go. Relax completely. Next, remove physical and other ills from your mind. Let your attention pass down the spinal cord and out over the nerves to the extremities, and as you do so, think: "My nerves are in perfect order all over my body. They obey my will, and I have

great nerve force." Next, bring your attention to the lungs and think: "I am breathing deeply and quietly, and the air goes into every cell of my lungs, which are in perfect condition. My blood is purified and made clean." Next, to the heart: "My heart is beating strongly and steadily, and my circulation is perfect, even to the extremities."

2) **Decree to the Body Function:** "My stomach and intestines perform their work perfectly. My food is digested and assimilated and my body rebuilt and nourished. My liver, kidneys, and bladder each perform their several functions without pain or strain; I am perfectly well. My body is resting, my mind is quiet, and my soul is at peace."

3) **Decree to the Mind:** "I have no anxiety about financial or other matters. God, who is within me, is also in all things I want, impelling them toward me; all that I want is already given to me. I have no anxiety about my health, for I am perfectly well. I have no worry or fear whatsoever. "I rise above all temptation to moral evil. I cast out all greed, selfishness, and narrow personal ambition; I do not hold envy, malice, or enmity toward any living soul. I will follow no course of action that is not in accord with my highest ideals. I am right and I will do right.'"

4) **Viewpoint Decree:** All is right with the world. It is perfect and advancing to completion. I will contemplate the facts of social, political, and industrial life only from this high viewpoint. Behold, it is all very good. I will see all human beings, all my acquaintances, friends, neighbors, and the members of my own household in the same way. They are all good. Nothing is wrong with the Universe; nothing can be wrong but my own

personal attitude, and henceforth I will keep that right. My whole trust is in God.

5) **Consecration**

I will obey my soul and be true to that within me that is highest. I will search within for the pure idea of right in all things, and when I find it I will express it in my outward life. I will abandon everything I have outgrown for the best I can think. I will have the highest thoughts concerning all my relationships, and my manner and action shall express these thoughts. I surrender my body to be ruled by my mind; I yield my mind to the dominion of my soul, and I give my soul to the guidance of God.

6) **Identification and Reconciliation**

There is but one substance and source, and of that I am made and with it I am one. It is my Father; I proceeded forth and came from it. My Father and I are one, and my Father is greater than I, and I do His will. I surrender myself to conscious unity with Pure Spirit; there is but one and that one is everywhere. I am one with the Eternal Consciousness.

7) **Idealization**

Form a mental picture of yourself as you want to be, and at the greatest height your imagination can picture. Dwell upon this for some little time, holding the thought: "This is what I really am; it is a picture of my own perfection and advancing to completion. I will contemplate the facts of social, political, and industrial life only from this high viewpoint. Behold, it is all very good. I will see all human beings, all my acquaintances, friends, neighbors, and the members of my own household in the same way. They are all good. Nothing is wrong with the Universe, nothing can be wrong but my own personal attitude, and henceforth I will keep that right. My whole trust is in God.

8) **Self Realization**

I appropriate to myself the power to become what I want to be, and to do what I want to do. I exercise creative energy; all the power there is, is mine. I will arise and go forth with power and perfect confidence; I will do mighty works in the strength of the Lord, my God. I will trust and not fear, for God is with me.

• Remember that simple pains and discomforts are sometimes signals to take action to better your physical health; however, many pains are the body at work healing and regenerating itself on a cellular and molecular level.

• As a note, you may be able to [work this positive Affirmation in your MIND for other people.]

• Do This Exercise every day for 30 days, print it out, memorize portions of it, and even add some of your own words to it. This exercise works miracles.

• ***This is an updated and expanded version of a Health Affirmation or Treatment taken from: The Science of Being Great" by Wattles – Elizabeth Towne Publishing 1914**

Strategy #4: Tune-Up the System – Getting Clear

Before you start focusing on your creative abilities and focusing on manifesting something new and concentrating on changing so much, sometimes you need to step back and take a hard look at your life, take a look at the last three, five, and 10 years, and analyze the successes and failures over this period. Begin an inventory of these years and discover the things that have been good for you and determine your actions and thinking that have not been constructive for you. Then what you need to do is learn to prune the tree for greater growth.

Learn to let go of the old things that haven't been useful and constructive for you, and then allow the things that have been good for you to stay and begin to cultivate these constructive activities. This will clear the slate and allow you to begin anew. Then, ultimately, you'll have more room in your heart and your mind to allow this new spiritual self, this new thinking or this fresh consciousness into your heart.

Now you may need to talk to a spiritual advisor or a life coach or a therapist or somebody licensed and qualified in these areas; you can talk through the old issues so that you can let go and get some closure and some catharsis from any old thoughts that are holding you back. But once you let go of all that junk, trim away all of that mental garbage, you will have created some spiritual space, some empty space in your mental garden to allow new beliefs and habits to flourish.

And here's the thing: the reason you want to process limiting beliefs is you don't want to have a mentality that is a "house divided." If you're dragging along a whole bunch of old baggage of negative thinking such as: resentments or anger or ego-related issues or hurt, there's got to be a way out of this. You've got to make a conscious decision to allow yourself to be helped, to allow your soul to let go of any negative past, because if you don't let go of all of the energy-sapping beliefs, you're going to have these old ideas tugging on your mind and it's going to be your old voice arguing with your new voice. As such, you don't want a house divided.

You want to be able to let go of that stuff so you can start fresh and get that reinvention that we have discussed. And if you have done the work and you've cleared away all the stuff that you don't want anymore in your life, there's going to be less distraction going forward, and you'll be more focused and you'll have more concentration and more controlled imagination. This newfound focus and optimism is what will ultimately help you propel yourself rapidly towards new heights and tranquility. Now, ultimately, if you go through this catharsis, then you've changed your view, you've changed your feelings, you've changed your imagination, and then guess what—you'll change your behavior and, miraculously, you'll change your outcomes.

Strategy #5: Claiming Mental Ownership & Worthiness

The next step involves really cultivating the feeling of having something already. So, to activate the power of assuming, all that we need to learn is to presuppose new destinies or assume success, but we also need to "mentally experience" that success. Thus, we have to change our essential concepts of ourselves and we have to persist in that desire to change until it is fact. We need to "Be that Ideal." We need to "feel the ideal outcome." We must sustain an attitude that we're open and receptive to the ideal. When I say ideal, I mean the ideal situation, the ideal result, the optimal outcome. So we need to surrender our intention to the new self, to the new essence, mentally, and capture the new ideal in our mind so that it becomes our dominant thought pattern and mental matrix.

We want a richer and fuller life. And ultimately our destiny is a result of our consciousness in the now, our consciousness *in the moment.* And most of the famous writers in prosperity and metaphysics will say that you have to form a mental image in your mind, on the picture screen in your mind, of what you desire or what you want to be, and then you need to learn to concentrate your attention upon this. And great teachers will say that before going to bed and when you wake up in the morning, you must gently think about this new mental picture of yourself, of how you want to be or what you want to achieve or the things you want to have. Think and feel as though you have it already in your heart and your mind. Cultivate that consciousness of having. And, when you nurture that consciousness of having the best, you're thinking from the position of owning it already, as if you were already there, in fact. Then ultimately your dominant emotions and mindset will be fuel for your creation of new forms and creation of new fortunes. And your determined imagination will help fill this vacuum.

For all of us, there comes a point in time when we make a conscious decision that we're not going to put up with the same old negative thinking, the same old scarcity thinking, the same old complaining. Extreme realism is what I would call it, where you're just so realistic that you are determined to be right about what's wrong. There comes a point when all of us wake up one morning and say, "We've got to let go of this." It is holding us back. So as soon as you make a conscious decision to control your thoughts and control your thinking and direct it towards constructive and productive ideals, then you'll be able to energize what you want to manifest in your life. You'll be able to give attention to the things that support your growth. And, you will be able to concentrate on your ideals and cultivate thanks for all the good and the lessons of the past. Then, you can begin to prune the old stuff "out of your life" and allow your imagination to expand to new levels.

And with this new thinking and this new constructive imagination, your dominant self-concept IS NOW *who you are*. This Dominant Mindset is what you will be. And you will have it, you'll use it, you'll feel it, and you will be it. Accordingly, your consciousness and your positive feelings regarding your becoming is what will generate your new ongoing reality. To do these things, you will have to sustain a receptiveness <u>in the now</u>, which will engender a new flow of creativity. As I said earlier, sometimes people don't even know what their purpose is supposed to be. Sometimes they don't even know what their burning desire is supposed to be. So when you clear away the mental rubbish and you become receptive, then you open yourself to this flow of creativity and ideas through your awareness and worthiness. And this manifestation of your ideas that are coming from this divine and spiritual flow will be your creation. That is your creative ability and where you find authentic desire and purpose.

To put it another way, your creativity is believing in the ideas that you have as presented in a form that already exists. And your assumptions and receptivity will allow for these preexisting mental forms to manifest themselves. And as I have intimated, your spiritual condition affects your perception and your worldview affects your experience and *raison d'être* or "reason to be," which is your true Purpose. Your ongoing conditioning is your power to manifest.

Strategy #6 - Acceptance and Gratitude – Mental Prosperity

First of all, acceptance is neither bad nor good; it's a little of both. In a sense, when you accept something, you're not just accepting what is wrong. You may be accepting what is well and good. So acceptance is really more of just surrender to what is. It's also being detached in a way that you're wearing life as a loose garment, and this detachment, just like Meister Eckhart said hundreds of years ago, allows you to be free and connected to the spirit of the universe or The Forces of GOD. And once you accept *what is* and realize that most distractions are merely material and external, you will see that the only true dominion and control that you must have is your internal consciousness, thinking, vibration, and character. And this positive acceptance can allow you to work on what is internal, the esoteric work, the inner growth, the building of yourself from the inside out, and that is the way that you change your thinking and change the way you see things and change your perception.   More importantly, if you can mentally accept the possibilities of good and greatness, then success is always a clear option in your mind and heart.

Let us look at it this way: if you change the way you feel about yourself, if you change your self-regard, you will change the way you see life and how you experience <u>everything</u>. And this is why a thankful heart or gratitude is so important for all of us. They say that belief and gratitude are probably the only pure antidotes to discouragement. Gratitude is the one power that if you exercise it every day in your life and you remain thankful in your heart for the ability to walk, talk, see, hear, think, create, it will reorganize your mindset into a state of thankfulness and connectedness to the creative power of the universe. It also breaks up the old preconceptions that are blocking you from that divine spiritual connection to the world and the universe, such as: greed, pride, lust, anger, gluttony, envy, sloth. Gratitude and belief also relieves you of the typical burdens such as resentment, jealousy, anger, and dissatisfaction. If you develop a sense of belief and knowingness based in gratitude, it will shatter negative mental concepts and allow the sunlight of the spirit to continue to shine upon you.

Strategy #7: Creative Visualization & Action

Napoleon Hill, Charles Haanel, and Wallace Wattles were probably the biggest selling authors of the 20th century in success, self help, and empowerment. They all said one thing very strongly, and they said that the clearer and more definite that you make the picture of your purpose/objective in your mind, the clearer you make your goal, the more vividly you can see it, the more you know what it looks like and what it feels like to have it, the better your chances are that that ideal or that thing will manifest itself in your life. And in the end, you've got to be able to see your desire and purpose vividly, you've got to be able to experience it in your mind, you've got to be grateful on the inside, in your heart, and you've got to cultivate a consciousness of having it, and cultivate a faith that it will be yours.

If you look at any Olympic athlete or professional athlete, whether it be basketball, football, track, or whatever it might be, all of these people are practicing every day, but they're also conditioning themselves mentally every day, and seeing themselves doing things every day in an excellent way. Whether it's putting a football across the goal, or putting a basketball through the net for a three-pointer, or running a marathon in a certain amount of time, these exceptional achievers strive to condition themselves mentally, and that's why seeing yourself doing something is key to a lot of success and is also a driver to ACTION. If you already have an idea that the wish can be fulfilled, then you already know that the goal can be accomplished. in addition, seeing each major step as accomplished is also a powerful exercise in incremental manifesting techniques.

In the bestseller, The Science of Getting Rich by Wattles, it stated, over a hundred years ago, "In order to get rich, you do not need a sweet hour of prayer; you need to pray without ceasing, and by prayer I mean holding steadily to your vision with the purpose to cause its creation into solid form and the faith that you are doing so." And remember, the best thing you can do for yourself, for your family, and for society and humanity is to make the best of yourself and to exercise your talents to their highest ability, because in the end that is what will allow you to give the most and help the greatest number of people.

Affirmative & Constructive Action

Taken as a whole, it is impossible for anyone to achieve his or her goals, his or her objectives, and his or her dreams without proficient <u>action</u>. How does anyone begin one thing and complete it? Keep in mind, every task has to begin with some act of boldness. As the famous Goethe stated, every idea or plan has to be initiated, and once you take that first step, you have taken an action towards the completion of that goal or attainment of that dream. So each day we have to do all we can to achieve that particular goal. We have to do all we can in the present moment and stay focused one step at a time, towards the incremental achievement of a particular objective. And I think that's what people mean by the concept of "24 hours a day." You don't have yesterday, you don't have tomorrow; what you have is today. All we have is right now and it's a gift, and if you can focus your mind and your attention on the actions that you need to do now and get them done effectively and efficiently, then you are destined to become great and destined to have a richer and fuller life.

If you don't know how to begin, take out a pen and paper and write down three things that you can do tomorrow, the three most important things that you can do tomorrow towards the attainment of your dream. And if you can't do all three tomorrow, it doesn't matter. But remember, each day you can do three things, for the betterment of yourself, the betterment of your family, and the betterment of society. And at the end of the day, if you do three things a day, you will have done over 1,000 actions in one year towards making yourself a better person, developing self-regard, building yourself up from the inside out, and at the end of one year, believe me, people will see the difference. Further, with writing, things down, this habit imprints aspirations on the sub-conscious to work on and sort out both while awake and sleeping. Thus, the process of writing down lists of tasks embeds the action plan in the mind so that ideas become a purpose-backed objective to work on, or at least to cultivate.

Being Excellent in Your Daily Activities

Many great writers talk about increase & value or giving without expectation, and all of these things are key virtues in the expansion and improvement of your life. What these authors mean by value and <u>increase</u> is that if you provide excellence to other people, then you will be known as excellent and a person who increases the lives of others. If you give someone quality service with that extra little something, go the extra mile, you will be remembered well by all people. And these acts, one by one, of excellence and increase in value, convey the impression to other people that you have the ability to provide advice, services, and products with skill, diligence, and enthusiasm. All of this adds up, and you will become rich in life, and you will become great, and you will become a shining star as a result of these metaphysical practices.

Chapter 3 - The Power of the Present - Presumption Decoded

Being Contemplative in Action – Getting Into NOW

If you have ever thought deeply about the magical power of the present moment, you may wonder if you have the capability for this type of superior focus and mindfulness. After reviewing all of the major religions on the philosophy of the power of PRESENCE, I have discovered many specific keys to success in being in the moment. To begin with, the theme of the Power of Awareness is to quiet the mind, calm the self-talk, and learn to control your thoughts while directing your thinking so that you may be present in the moment, to be alive and conscious "right now."

This is not necessarily an Eastern or Western concept; however, there are many esoteric and Christian underpinnings herein that are addressed. Firstly, it is advised that we intently listen to our self-talk deep within our mind and then try to truly see and listen to that inner voice as an observer. Getting to know your ego voice as compared to the authentic spiritual voice of your heart is also a major exercise of this topic.

The easiest example of directing your awareness to the now is to direct your controlled attentiveness to your body, to your breathing, to what you see, what you hear, what you're eating or what you're tasting or who you're with. Whether it's focusing on the aliveness of your child or actually seeing or sensing parts of your own body, you can go deeper into your awareness. Here's an example: Try to actually feel your extremities, actually noticing the feelings in your fingers or feelings in your toes at any given moment. Or, what emotions are going on in your mind or even in your stomach.

If you're like the average person, your mind could be harping on 50 different things at once, like a TV on 50 different channels constantly running, and the real key is to pick a channel and focus on a single concept, one thing at a time, one moment at a time, one day at a time, one instance at a time. Further, we can concentrate on one thing at a time, or we can just be aware of the moment and allow our mind to do what is best for us. As an example, in the famous movie *The Last Samurai* with Tom Cruise, it talks about no mind. To NOT overthink everything is what a teacher would mean by no mind, not overanalyzing every single move or every single tactic. And just like driving, the first time you drive the car or use stick shift, there's many things that you're learning how to do that sooner or later become something embedded in your subconscious or in your machinery, and you automatically can get in a car and know exactly what you need to do. So the key really is to be able to program the way you live to think and live in a way that doesn't require you to overanalyze everything. This process allows you to exist in your real-time state of aliveness.

After rereading books on mysticism and self-empowerment, many of us have an awakening of consciousness, a spiritual awakening of sorts, and don't even know how it happened or what had happened, and years later we figure out that as a byproduct of reading what other mystics had taught about these types of transformations, we became better people.

However, there are many of us out here in the world who have already had this similar type of awakening, this aliveness, this consciousness, and if you are one of us, you know it deeply. If you're on an enlightened path, you will inherently know it because you can walk into a room with 100 people in it, and you can look around and you actually see people and you're actually alive and you actually know what is happening. And if you're living in this awake-ness, you will have the ability to control what's going on in your mind and your thoughts, and you will have the ability to choose and decide the type of thinking that you will have all day long. In the end, the type of thinking that you have all day long, the type of actions you do all day long, IS the person who you ARE, who you are becoming. Then that's who and what you REALLY are. That is what you will become.

So, in total, if you're able to control your thinking and you're able to control who you are and the totality of your actions and inactions, then you're entirely able to control your destiny and you're able to control what you become.

In books such as Meditations by Marcus Aurelius, On Detachment by Meister Eckhart, or *The Power of Now* by Eckhart Tolle, the authors discuss key issues such as: "detachment", "no mind" and "pain body." And I'm going to explain the concept to you right now. Detachment may be a simple way of saying the following: If you are a person who is sitting around each day thinking negative & destructive thoughts, trying to be the victim and trying to identify with all this unfairness, your mind id clouded with pain. If you complain all of the time while also trying to blame everyone except yourself for their situation, that is the pain body. You can learn about ego-related psychological issues in: church, in therapy, in temples, from a life coach, or in various spiritual venues.

And what I'm saying is that if you have this ego that's wrapped up in its own identity and it's trying to protect itself, it's not going to want to take a look in the mirror. Your ego is not going to want to change. It's not going to want to accept responsibility for your life and the way you are and what's become of you. So if you can break free of that bondage, you can find your spiritual self, your true inner self, who you really are and get in touch with that and get in touch with the spirituality within, then all of a sudden this unlimited flow and this unlimited potentiality becomes available to you, and that's where this aliveness comes from. And that's what the Christians talk about as being *contemplative in action.* Christians also talk about the Holy Spirit, which is basically that connectedness and that non-separateness, that *spiritual, god-unity* that every faith around the world speaks of in relation to illumination.

Once you enter this aliveness and this newfound awakening in consciousness, you'll have no need to constantly defend yourself mentally or overtly. You'll have no desire to overreact to things. You'll have this true power within. And also you'll have this new consciousness, which determines how you effectively manifest life's journey. By and large, if you're able to develop a new consciousness of aliveness, a higher consciousness of success, a greater consciousness of action and doing things, this _**"in the moment"**_ consciousness is what will transmute ideas into success and transform possibility into mental form, bringing ideas into material, tangible form on this earthly plane.

In many other religions or spiritual movements, you'll hear the word "acceptance" and being able to accept what is. Groups may espouse, "Accept the now or accept the good or accept the bad and let go of it." Generally, this is what will free you from the present attitude that is saying that you should struggle or be a victim. Furthermore, this bold idea of knowingness is what you really want. You want to know and believe that you could control your destiny, and if you don't know and you don't believe, then you might be sitting around wishing for something to happen or hoping for something to happen, and it can keep you stuck in the past, or in the future.

False hope can keep you from realizing your dreams if your ego and your "self" is so identified with what is wrong with YOUR world. If you can change your train of thought and change how you think, you'll be able to allow your mind to focus on what is right with the world and look at what is good and what is beautiful. And if you start focusing on all the good and the beauty or the _rightness_ and the righteousness of the world along with the universe's impersonal laws and bountiful nature, you'll be able to see and attract more of what is good, right, and wholesome into your stream of thought.

In essence, your personal development and self-regard is an inside job. Transformation to a higher order is a quantum-spiritual-science. This mystical power is also the power of consciousness and being connected. So being able to control what goes on inside your consciousness is esoteric and this science is what spiritual and religious and philosophical leaders have been talking about since Pythagoras, Socrates, Plato, Confucius, Buddha, Aristotle, and all the rest. The great teachers have been talking about these metaphysical-scientific concepts since the beginning of civilization. If you can master yourself, you'll be able to master your destiny and have a great effect upon those around you while also doing a great service for humanity.

The sheer benefits of "The Power of Consciousness" or being aware "in the present moment" are these facts: This power allows you to compartmentalize the day, which keeps you from being paralyzed by any non-urgent situations, and you're able to free the mind of attachments. And if you can free the mind of too much junk that's floating around in it, you're able to focus and concentrate and direct your energies into the areas that will most improve your life from the inside out.

Additionally, attention is energy, so you need to remember what you focus on expands in your life. You need to choose and decide what to energize with your attention in any given moment. So like I said before, the pain body is this negative energy of the ego mind, and if you're able to get your attention away from that and give your attention to things that are constructive and positive and reinvigorating, then that's what you want to do because if you give your attention to the pain body, guess what? That's fuel that will keep pain flowing and going. Those who teach about the power of the PRESENT also write a lot about how your conscious mind and your subconscious mind coexist, or rather, how to transcend your ego self to begin to listen to your spiritual voice.

It's like this: all of us really need to tap into our spiritual self, which is basically the best friend that you always as a child. Now you know that there's an old adage that says that some children have their little best friend, their *imaginary* friend, which is really their spiritual-higher-self that they are embracing and befriending, and their imagination allows them to love that part of their "spiritual self" without limitation. This connection allows many to be connected to their authentic voice. However, a lot of children lose this magical relationship at a very early age.

We know this story. We've seen it time and time again, so we know that this spiritual self, this best friend, that's the authentic relationship that we need to cultivate. The relationship with our spiritual self and our relationship with the *spirit of the universe* should come first for us so that we may maximize our peace and prosperity.

Some of these famous authors of "days gone by" have said that when you have a grateful mind and a thankful heart, it is a lot easier to maintain a living faith. Thus a mind of joy cannot support a "blame/victim mindset" or negative thinking. So the best thing that we can all do for ourselves to change our worldview is to revolutionize how we think and change our state of gratefulness. As the famous philosopher Magus Incognito once said, each person's worldview is based on his or her spiritual condition, and this worldview hinges on the gratitude and faith that we cultivate.

So the word "alchemy" really means transmuting one substance into another substance, and if you could transform your lower self into your higher self thinking, if you could transcend from your ego toward your spiritual essence, that is the real key to these teachings. Transmutation is achieved by the conscious unity with the spirit of the universe. Transmutation is achieved through the consciousness of love, the consciousness of wisdom, the consciousness of gratitude and joy.

The next issue in the power of the moment is how many of us are addicted to the adrenaline of anger, self-righteousness, justified anger, and blame. Unfortunately that's why social justice has become such a trendy thing—because it can get you so riled up about blaming somebody for something that happened a long time ago when in essence if we focused all that very same time and energy on inner social justice, our views of society would transform. Thus, the whole world consciousness would probably change for the better.

And the other thing is that we can get obsessed with negativity if we surround ourselves with angry people, people who are not alive with faith, people who are pessimistic-realists, or who think the whole world is bad. This type of attitude is contagious, and regrettably, as spiritual seekers, we want to be close to those who want a spiritual life. And if we can draw close to those who have the same general desire of wholeness and aliveness and health, then we will all become healthier much quicker, and this of course is why self-help groups and fellowships of all sorts have become so popular over the last 30, 40, 50 years. This earnest desire for healing, faith, wholeness, and happiness constitutes a curative vibration that has been proven to put various diseases into remission.

The theme of "Real Time Consciousness" is correlated to being in flow and allowing detachment. The great Rhineland Mystic, Meister Eckhart, talked a lot about detachment. And we're talking about non-resistance and being in tune with Spirit, and there's just so many times in our lives when we can just let go, stay connected, and thrive. Accordingly, some of the biggest miracles in our lives happen when we're not fighting something, we have our mouths shut, and we just allow things to unfold. We have to know when to FLOW and when to pick our battles and know when to stand up for ourselves, but, in general, 99 percent of the time we're going to be okay if we can just stay calm, do our best in the moment, and allow people just to be.

Once you have developed this aliveness, this consciousness, & this higher order in your life, you will know what it feels like and you're going to want more of this genuine exhilaration. You're going to do the things that you must do to stay in tune and embrace and own this newfound power, because it feels so good to be alive and to be clear. Further, if we keep our minds somewhat clear and we do the things we need to do each day or each week to maintain that spirit, that clarity and that peace of mind will be available and afforded to us.

In the end, this chapter is about surrender. It's about "surrendering to win." If you let go of the things that are hurting you, you will be able to move forward where you do not need to drag around a lot of dead weight along with you anymore. You will be more free, more clear and more nimble   And then you'll learn to act with purpose and clarity and focus because you're not carrying all this excess baggage. And then you'll learn to do all you can in the now. And this surrender really unveils your spiritual power.

So, in essence, a lot of religions, movements, and spiritual groups talk about this key to power of freeing and clearing the mind. When you're able to master yourself, you're able to let go of all the junk from the past, you're able to create this space inside of you and allow joy, faith, wholeness, and greatness to come into your heart for the first time.

Some people refer to this process as creating a spiritual vacuum, and this vacuum, once you have cleared away the old mental baggage, creates space where something has to fill it.   This is where the miracle begins and you can fill the space with love, aliveness, joy, and enthusiasm And if you're in the "power of the moment" and you have this consciousness of good where you believe and you know that the world will take care of you in spite of everything that's going on, then good things will come to you. Good people, good ideas, good opportunities, good health, and so forth will all be available to you.

So, in summary, this new Consciousness involves developing a relaxed and free awareness of the now, IN the moment. In this higher awareness, you may now become receptive and awake to the good and the beautiful things in the world such as gratitude, health, aliveness, optimism, knowingness, and your "I am-ness" where your "spiritual and divine energy/presence" is made available to you. And what is the "I am?" The "I am" is your presence where you know you are connected to power. It is your *unified spirit* that is talked about in the old wisdom literature.

For many seekers, this is the moment of transformation, when you wake up one morning, after having been engaging gratitude in your daily life, and you are free from the mental baggage of your past and you are consciously using these methods and these steps of developing clarity,

And behold, one morning thereafter, YOU WAKE UP, and you're MENTALLY on the RIGHT side of the bed. And then a few days later, if you keep practicing this consciousness of love and consciousness of God and consciousness of gratitude, you wake up again like that. Then, all of a sudden you'll continue to wake up on the right side of the bed for a few consecutive days, and you now look forward to the days and you'll be alive and want to do things each day for yourself and other people and participate in life. And thus, you go from hope to faith, and from faith to KNOWING. And all of this aliveness and that now-ness and that spiritual awake-ness is what dissipates this pain body and this negative thinking.

So, in conclusion, you and a lot of other people, once you become awake, you're going to be so thrilled and energized by it that you're going to feel reinvented. You're going to want to repudiate generalized negative thinking, and if you hear other people talking about negative thinking and pessimistic stuff and wasteful stuff, you're not going to want to be around them.

What I'm saying, if you hear your own voice in your mind and you're observing your mind complaining and trying to justify and blame, you will be inclined to tell it to stop. You're going to want to wake up to be alive, in tune with the infinite and connected to the world, and you're going to want to be aware to see the beauty of life, regardless of what bad things happen.

Un fortunately, we all have had some big challenges in life.... I've gone through tragedies like Hurricane Katrina. I've lost loved ones, including close family members. I've lost businesses, had greedy people steal from me, and I've had burdens just like everyone else. I've had losses and defeats and pain and real catastrophic events in my life, but when you achieve this aliveness and this consciousness of now, you know that you can move on and you can prevail to go to greater heights regardless of what happens. This is because you truly have yourself and you have your unity, your empowerment, and your earnest connection to the Spirit of the Universe.

Chapter 4- The Twelve-Fold Path of Prosperity ™

In this age of a fast-paced and high-tech world, people are, more and more, seeking a strategic path to: authentic health, inner peace, better careers, and success. Becoming a warrior at true peace with yourself is the first key to happiness. Bridging your actions to your spiritual mind and body is where success can naturally emerge. To manifest a greater destiny, a person must make an informed inventory of their assets and desires. Each of us must 1) Analyze the results of our recent track record 2) Make a diagnosis of what tactics are good or bad 3) Create a plan to improve our lives on mental, physical and spiritual levels 4) Implement the new strategic actions 5) Monitor the ongoing results 6) Take corrective measures from time to time.   To implement a new plan, we must form a clear and definite mental image of the results that he or she wishes to have, to achieve, or see the ideal image of what he or she wants to become. The seeker must cultivate his or her new beliefs using a higher order of imagination so as to feel worthy of greater heights. Throughout these 12 steps below, we will discuss the twelve keys to joy, flow, excellence, peace, and abundance. The person who wants to have an abundant life and prosperity must accurately develop his or her purpose and learn to imagine living the life that he or she would want to live. A true seeker of prosperity will learn to see their presumed destinies with an earnest thanksgiving that his new reality is manifesting.

This is the methodology by which mental energy or mental impressions are transferred over to the universe, and the creative forces are set in motion like a tiny chain reaction of activity. Each of us must use proper attention and concentration intertwined with harmonious mind, faith, and gratitude that is all rooted in love. Your higher consciousness will then begin working with you to allow greater attention, concentration, and natural expression on a higher level. Defining your purpose in life or aiming toward specific outcomes while letting them unfold in the best ways will be where the miracles appear. Moreover, allowing your talents, true place, and right career to expand will also be a powerful part of your journey. Ultimately, developing stronger: concentration, thoughts, speech, and a greater worldview to support your actions and goals will be the catalyst of newfound successes. Combining the awakened mind with action is where your results begin to appear and build momentum towards tremendous growth and expansion.

1. Constructive Motives with Attentiveness

The first principles of the path, attention and concentration, are described as a laser focusing of the mind, which is a state in which all cognitive faculties are unified and directed to a particular objective. This is not simply being aware of your environment, but being conscious of your thought energy. By thinking, an earnest desire is brought to you, and by acting, you bring the desire into reality. While staying focused with faith and purpose, imagine your desired objective with all your heart and with all your strength, and with all your concentration. Hold the vision of yourself with the highest and best result on the picture screen of your mind. Next, use your current abilities or position as a means of developing yourself and continuous improvement. Keeping a vision of your purpose or goal held with confident expectation and purpose will cause the universe to move toward you with the right possibilities for your growth. Further, your action, if performed in the light of the intention of harmony and concentration, will bring you continuous, creative opportunity. See the life that you want as if it is pure possibility and as part of your essence. See yourself in possession of the life and abilities that you so desire. Make use of them in your imagination as if

they are your present reality. Meditate upon your purpose
and vision until it is clear and distinct, and then take the
mental attitude of ownership toward everything in that
picture. Take possession of success in your mind, in the full
belief that is truly yours. Hold to this vision and do not waiver
in your belief that what you desire is yours in heart and mind.
And remember to be thankful for blessings received and new
inspiration "at all times," as you would when it has taken
form. If we can thank the universe for what is imagined in the
mind, we will have prosperity and peace, and we will become
co-creators of everything that we earnestly want.

Remaining contemplative in action is also part of being in the
moment. Your awareness is your "Life Force Consciousness."
With focus and refinement of mind, your awake-ness will be
natural and potent. You will see and sense new ideas and feel
the power of intuition and knowingness. You will recognize
when to act and how to act, and you will be in tune with the
infinite.

2. Higher Purpose in the World

Everyone should engage in a career and occupation that he or she
enjoys in a spiritual and productive way. All persons can follow
their dreams and exercise their God-given talents in a way that
naturally expresses their life force. Therefore, we should be able to
feel proud of our work while being rewarded for what we have
created and produced for others. This is the law of compensation
and flow. A higher purpose involves win-win relationships in which
everyone benefits. Our work can be for the good of all those
involved, where everyone gets some kind of increase in their lives
due to operating with higher purpose. Before becoming fearful of
ambition, realize that poverty, misery, and sacrifice are not pleasing

to anyone. Ambition is merely a desire to adapt, grow, and create.
In contrast, pretending to be poor, charitable, or miserable to
achieve attention is a losing proposition. Remember that extreme
altruism is no better and no nobler than extreme selfishness, where
both are forms of greed. Thus, we can and must believe in the
possibility of growth, wealth, and prosperity. As such, we do not
have to entertain the idea of scarcity or competition. To achieve
abundance, we must create and innovate. We must become who we
are supposed to be and there is no need to compete for the little
scraps of food from the table when abundance is plentiful. You
know people who work in a field of joy who prosper, and you can do
this also. You do not have to take anything from anyone. You do not
have to cheat, steal, or take advantage in negotiations. You can
operate from a win-win perspective where all benefit from your
contributions. You must become a creator, not a competitor, and
you will get what you want, but in such a way that each person will
have more because of your actions.

3. Specificity of Vision & Contemplation

Contemplation of your intentions is similar to planting the seed of
your vision or purpose. If we are definite in our intentions and
purpose, our dreams can unfold along the lines of our true path.
Writing down our intentions is also magical, and has a superb
effect, especially in clarifying our direction and goals to ourselves
and upon our subconscious mind.   However, it is in our mindset
that we cultivate what we really want. In order to coalesce our
consciousness toward any direction, we must "focus relentlessly
during all hours." And this means holding constant attention to
your vision, with the intent to cause the transformation of our ideas
into form. We can operate on a plane of mental harmony and good
will, and we can flow constructively with life. It is better not to resist

potentiality. We can allow life to unfold in conjunction with our constructive and faithful action. We can make the best of ourselves while in a state of peace and wellbeing. Our highest truth is harmony, bliss, health, and success.

4. Strategic Communication

Safeguard your communications both internally and externally. We should NOT speak of ourselves or our affairs unless with confidants who desire success for us. Never talk about life, career, or the economy as sad, or business conditions as terrible. Times may be hard but business is only bad for those who are operating with a scarcity consciousness.

Remember, you are a constructive creator, your ideas help people, your ideas do not take away from anyone, you can create what you want, and you are above fear. When others are having hard times and poor business, you will find your greatest opportunities. Right communication means the way you talk to others and to yourself. Train yourself to think and speak of life getting better and better with unlimited supply. Always speak in terms of forward movement; to do otherwise is to deny your faith.

5. Bold, Efficient Action

Every action that we take is either productive or ineffective. Each inefficient action is non-productive, and if you spend your life doing inefficient things, you will not enjoy peace or success. The more wasteful things that you do, the worse for you. On the other hand, if your every action is constructive, and if every act of your life is efficient, your whole life will be successful. The causation of failures is doing things in an inefficient manner without focus, and not doing enough things in an efficient manner. You will see that it is a self-evident proposition that if you avoid inefficient acts, and if you do a sufficient number of constructive acts each day, you will enjoy a richer and fuller life.

Every action that is backed by an earnest desire must be strong. Every act can be made strong by contemplating or knowing your purpose while you are doing it. If you also put all the power of love, faith, and gratitude in your action, it can further magnify your power and focus. Ultimately, we must create the means to capture, receive, and harvest the fruits that life offers to us so that we can use it for our development and also help mankind. While these steps force creation into motion, your desires may not appear according to your specific wants but rather manifest in a greater or more appropriate outcome at a later date. Never allow yourself to feel disappointed if this is the case. You can expect to have a certain thing at a certain time, but not get it at that time, and it will appear as a loss. But if you hold to your faith, you will find that the failure is only temporary. It may be a lesson to take a fresh path. If you do not receive the desired outcome, you may soon get something much better, and you will see that the apparent loss was really a great success.

6. Harmonious Mind

Mindfulness is the controlled and perfected faculty of cognition. It is the mental ability to see beyond what is apparent with clear consciousness.   To do this, you must acquire the ability to think the way you want to think. This is the first step towards achieving abundance. Thinking what you want to think is controlling your mental imagery and inner voice, which is enabling truth regardless of appearances. Every person has the natural and inherent power to think what he or she wants to think with practice. Seeing past what seems evident is possible if you are willing to train yourself and allow yourself to grow on a spiritual and metaphysical level. The more you can harmoniously focus your mind while imagining all of your goal's details, the better. This will bring the Supreme Force into accord with your highest good where the Universe must cooperate with you. Mental harmony also implies that we should be aware that others on this earth are here to help us and may offer assistance. We should be in tune with these opportunities that may come from many places in the form of other people seeking us out. Harmony is achieved and cultivated by keeping your mind clear of confusion, where it has room to allow flow and goodness to freely enter.

7. Effective Comprehension – Understanding

This means seeing, understanding, interpreting. and believing the highest truth. At our lowest level of existence, we see all things as misery and suffering. We can achieve a higher order of living if we can see life as a miracle and go beyond what the critical mind can see. Having the correct view provides peace of mind, the ability to act, the enhanced possibility of good fortune, and a sense of wellbeing. In the same vein, we manifest internally and externally the thoughts that we think about all day. So our views and how we focus our attention are extremely important. Thinking ideas of abundance, health, love, and so on, is a force much greater than any negative ideas. Sometimes, the correct interpretation of our next move is simply doing what is ahead of us, one thing at a time, with excellence, and doing things right the first time. For higher understanding, we develop a state of mind that is conducive to our desires. We direct positive thoughts, enthusiasm, belief, and persistence to be built on truth. Truth can be perceived in a constructive way or we can base our truth on lack or negativity. We all know that a bitter and negative attitude is not an effective way to live and can actually program persons for failure. As they say, *"Realists Expect Failure & Demand to Be Right."* Seeing constructive potentiality takes skill and practice. When exercising the principles of a comprehensive awareness, you will expand this skill over time.

8. Joyful Effort

Having a sense of flow with your work and endeavors can be seen as a reward from utilizing a combination of the principles of the 12-fold path. Nothing can be achieved without effort, which is in itself an act of will, whereas non-definite effort distracts the mind from its task, and confusion may be the consequence. Thus, you must really desire prosperity in your work life. This, in effect, can be compared to detached but focused activity, where you are flowing with the universe with non-resistance of mind.

The clearer and more definite you see yourself in flow and success, the stronger your effort will become, and the stronger your power, the easier it will be to hold your mental energy fixed upon the outcome of what you yearn for. Behind your earnest and specific vision must be the essence to realize and recognize it, to bring it into corporeal expression. Right efforts mixed with confident expectation or faith will become natural productivity animated with results. Behind this intention must be an invincible and unwavering belief that the reward is already yours and that you already have it in possession in your mind's eye. Thus, you need only to take ownership of it psychologically and accept it with an open mind to own it. Live in the new objective, mentally, until it takes form around you physically. No haste is required. However, we know energy is more effective with preparedness. Even the mighty Lincoln said that if he had eight hours to cut down a tree, he would spend six sharpening the axe. Thus, being ready in your mind, body, and Spirit can enable a seamless flow of action. In the mental realm, enter into full enjoyment of the things you want. "Whatsoever things ye ask for when ye pray, believe that ye receive them, and ye shall have them," said The Great Master.

9. **Open to Receive Inspiration**

Many people from around the world feel unworthy of abundance. Many do not value themselves, their abilities, their talents, or their work. It is very important to learn to feel worthy and deserving of good. You are a unique and spiritual being created by the universe with a celestial purpose. As a unique being in communion with the universal flow of ideas, you should become mentally open to receiving all good things in life. Further, people should be careful to allow the receipt of blessings into their lives from the Universe and from others. *Example*: Accepting a compliment from another person or having a method of being rewarded financially.

True and lasting Prosperity has a spiritual foundation that includes balance. Successful persons master excellence in body, mind, and spirit. When there is balance, ideas and energy flow from the universe to the person who is exercising this higher realm of existence. When we are at our best and acting as spiritually effective individuals, we actually have more ideas flowing to us from the "universal mind" or consciousness of the infinite.

Therefore, we can participate in our destiny and co-create our own reality. If you read the great spiritual minds of the Renaissance, you will quickly see that it is the right of the individual to have a direct experience with the Deity of your understanding through prayer, meditation, and getting back to the spiritual basics. Taking quiet time to meditate, pray or contemplate, may indeed create an untold mystical flow of inspiration to all who try.

10. Gratitude and Belief – The Vibration

Gratitude and Thankfulness lead to greater constructive expectation in our daily living. Positive expectation and confident expectation that is based in belief IS THE SUBSTANCE OF FAITH.

Recognize possibility, praise others, bless others, and bless and praise yourself. Blended with humility, your harmonious connection to universal spirit will allow a pipeline of grace to flow upon you. A thankful heart is highly conducive to faith, bliss, and living with joy. Realize that you are free to create abundance and that you are worthy of the gifts of the universe. With your higher belief, you free your mind's mental and spiritual power to focus on what you want. What you think about becomes expansive in your life. Your focus on the good and the great will bring these miracles into your world.

Faith and Belief are the deciding energy in many situations. All things created equal, the scientific probability of a coin toss result is 50 percent in its purest form. However, it only takes a grain of sand to tilt the balance of a scale in one direction. Thus, something as small as a mustard seed on one side of the balance can, in fact, lean the probability of prosperity in one direction versus another. In sum, the cosmic cards can begin to be dealt in your favor with the influence of intention and gratitude. In the end, happiness and gratitude are reasonable options that lead to the greater possibility of success and peace of mind.

11. **Love Energy and Forgiveness**

Love is the quality of thought and emotion that will propel us into a state of bliss and achievement.

Love all there is. Focus on the good, the great, the constructive, and the beauty of life. See the best in all there is. Look for the good that occurs in the world.

Meditate on the people who have been kind to you, the creation all around you, the good that happens every day, the inventions for the betterment of humanity, and the positive happenings around the world that occur each and every day. Learn to love all and love yourself, and love will be attracted to you. Love is a composite of many things including gratitude, harmlessness, peace, kindness, and compassion. Thinking love and giving love will liberate you into the fourth dimension of harmony. Think of how you have already been blessed, protected, and guided throughout your life. Yes, lessons have been learned, and further happiness, peace, and success may be yours if you stay on the path of quantum bliss.

Cultivating love and forgiveness can dispel otherwise discouraging thoughts. Great minds can look back on things they love or loved, and recapture that emotion. Empower yourself and your spiritual self with love, gratitude, kindness, harmonious thinking, harmless action, and serenity. Your dreams will be realized as long as you do not resist the gifts of abundance and remain aware of life's gifts.

Contemplate the concepts of St. Paul: Patience, Kindness, Understanding, Generosity, Sincerity, Humility, Gentleness ... Love never Fails.

12. **Wisdom - Having these qualities: Knowledge Perception**

Wisdom is said to be composed of the qualities of: experience, knowledge, and good judgment. Acting with wisdom is said to be the path of prosperity. Having money, good looks, or power is not necessary, but having wisdom is a requirement for health, happiness, and success. As they say, a man with money meets a man with experience, and the man with the money gets an experience, and the man with experience ends up with the money.

Having the power to picture potentiality and make healthy decisions and winning choices will create a life of prosperity and abundance. While wisdom is crucial, acting upon it is also the mother of the greatest successes in history.

* These concepts from *The 12-Fold Path* are inspired by the combined teachings of many great masters such as: Pythagoras, Marcus Aurelius, Schopenhauer, Hegel, Swedenborg, Emerson, Napoleon Hill, William Walker Atkinson, Charles Haanel, Genevieve Behrend, Epicurean Thought, Stoicism, Taoism, Confucianism, Thoreau, and W. Wattles. Everything is possible with desire, faith, love, harmonious action, and constructive thinking. Remember that these are important steps in our pursuit of excellence and peace. Take the best ideas from the list and use them to improve your life:

Chapter 5: Shangri La Warrior Spiritual and Success Exercises

1. **Visualize Your Day -** At night, review your day – hour by hour. Try to remember what you did from the time you woke up to the end of the day. See each event, each interaction, each relationship. After visualization, consider the things that you could have done better. With this precept of order, much like the spiritual exercises of Ben Franklin over 200 years ago, you may build your character as well as your imagination skills each day.

2. **Contemplative Prayer -** Prayer, breath-work, meditation, visualization, and recognition of health and peace can be taken point by point through the body using a quasi-chakra observance system. When doing the health exercises in this book, you also imagine a healing light going through each chakra region.

Exercise: Sit in a chair or lie down. Close your eyes. Take in air through your nose, hold it for seven seconds, and then let it out of your mouth slowly. Do this at least three times to enter a relaxed state. Clench your fists and extend your fingers as far as they will go a few times and put your hands in your lap. Now clear your mind and imagine a peaceful scene such as a mountain meadow with flowers or a calm lake. Now, begin with the top of your head or crown, or you can also begin with the base or lower body. Go through each of the seven sections in one direction. The first letters of the colors are ROY.G.BIV (red, orange, yellow, green, blue, indigo, violet) with red beginning with the lower body and the head/crown corresponding to the color violet.

Now, go through all seven colors one by one, imaging the color of each chakra and the corresponding section of the body. Imagine each color purifying and regenerating the body, one by one. Relax and purify each section of the body one by one. When you have finished the exercise from crown to lower or lower to higher, release any impure energy to the universe while taking a few breaths from the nose and blowing out from the mouth. Then, express a mental thanks to the Supreme for the healing energy. Then open your eyes.

1. Muladhara (Sanskrit: Mūlādhāra) Lower body - our connection to the earth and the physical plane – Survival and Operation – Color: Red
2. Swadhisthana (Sanskrit: Svādhisthāna) Reproductive gland region of the body – our creative and procreative urges and drives – Color: Orange
3. Manipura (Sanskrit: Manipūra) Stomach/navel - energy center for power and manifestation and desires (location: solar plexus) – Color: Yellow
4. Anahata (Sanskrit: Anāhata) Heart - energy center for love – Color: Green
5. Vishuddha (Sanskrit: Viśuddha) Throat - center for expression – Color: Blue
6. Ajna (Sanskrit: Ājñā) Eyebrow or forehead between brows - our psychic powers – Color: Indigo
7. Sahasrara (Sanskrit: Sahasrāra) Top of head and crown - connection with the Cosmic or the divine. – Color: Violet

3. **Breathing and Purification** – Try to learn the purification breath work. Breathe slowly into your nose and out from your mouth. Imagine negative energy leaving your body with each exhale and see yourself with each intake
breath taking in life, love, pure energy, and healing elements.

4. **Sensory Perception** – Learn to feel each part of the body uniquely. Sit or lie down and close your eyes. Then, pick a part of your body. Sense it, feel it, imagine where it is. If a part of your body has aches, pains, or dis-ease, then use this exercise to send healing energy to that spot in a targeted way.

5. **Constructive Journaling** – Every month or every three to six months, sit down and write out things that you are proud of. Write 10 things that you have done to improve your life in recent months. List your best attributes. Write out 5-10 things that you enjoy doing or would like to try. List things that you can do to respect yourself. Even write out a few luxury to-dos where you can take action each year to treat yourself to a trip, family fun, to luxury, or to learning.

6. **COT: Cognitive Occupational Therapy** – Every few days or weeks, you must do things that are cognitive and that involve neuroplasticity exercises. Examples are: learning to recite a poem or prayer, working puzzles, crosswords, or even chores such as unloading the dishwasher, building a model, writing a story, telling a story, preparing and giving a presentation or related activities. The "mind-hand" or "mind-speech" activity is very stimulating and builds mental muscle.

7. **Vibration** - Your vibration can be at many levels. To say the least, you can enhance your mental vibration through various actions. Higher levels of mental and spiritual vibrations include Love, Gratitude, Praise, Faith, Feel Good Emotions, and more. Many practitioners work on a daily basis to enhance and bring their mental and spiritual vibration to a higher level. Practitioners do this so that they may lead a more harmonious life, but also to attract people, events, and things of the same or higher vibration. The end result of

healthy vibrations is the attraction of more constructive events, outcomes, and possibilities.

8. **Euphoric Modeling** – Recall a certain past event or image that brings feelings of joy, happiness, peace, love, or endearment. Have this MOMENT at your beck and call. Whenever you feel a pestering negative thought, seize upon the moment of peace and seek out solutions, forgiveness, and peace of mind.

9. **Cause and Effect** - For every thought, action, or inaction, there is a corresponding thought and event. Your heartfelt emotions when mixed with constructive thought and action carry more force than the average thought and action. Building a foundation is vital to this step. At first, we must change our mentality from one of lack to a consciousness and mind of possibility. Our minds and hearts evolve and begin to believe in opportunity and abundance. Instead of thinking why, we transcend to a spiritual position of why not. At this juncture, we begin to take action in accordance with our dreams. Each mental and physical action we take on a daily basis adds to the momentum of our spiritual force. Our spiritual force in conjunction with our harmonious and constructive thinking begins to manifest higher realities in our days to come.

10.   **Habits and Routines** – Develop healthier routines by seeking out activities that build your life and improve your circumstances. Learn to reward yourself for superior habits. Sit down with a trusted advisor and analyze your daily routines. Review your rituals, what you watch, how you exercise, how you think, where you go, who you associate with, what you do to respect yourself.   Evaluate all of these things and then determine how to better treat yourself to a life of excellence, self-regard, transformation, and fewer distractions.

Chapter 6 – Shangri-La Laws of Success

Key Metaphysical Laws and Philosophical Concepts

Harmonious Relationships:

Connected with all there is that is good, harvesting and having a harmonious relationship with the world through various philosophical exercises, using gratitude for any of your gifts on a daily basis can grow your expectation of good and faith. It is much easier to be connected when you have set aside or removed destructive thinking such as resentments, jealously or the seven deadly sins.

Desires

Desires are good and excellent. Desires can focus you on enriching your life and following your true direction. Cultivating desires into reality is vital for change, innovation, and improvement. You would not have a desire unless it was possible, but select desires where you have a solid sphere of possibility. An earnest and heartfelt desire is what allows us to seize upon opportunities and develop plans.

Plans

A plan or objective is fundamental in the clarification and specificity of your desire. A large majority of people are afraid to specify what they intend to do. Transcending this fear and taking bold action upon your plans and strategies allows for the growth and manifestation of your idea into a reality

Vision

A vision is important in that you clarify the path to your short-term and long-term enrichment of yourself, your goals, teamwork, or relationships.

Mission

A mission is important in that you can quantify and clarify a path to an outcome or ending strategy.

Having, Emotion, and Feelings

Mentally understanding the outcome or result as if you have it already is very important. It also allows you to qualify the consequences. It further provides you with feelings surrounding the outcome. Harvesting positive feelings surrounding the outcome is very important to energize a desire, mission, visualization, and result.

Visualization, Pictures, Imagination, Sending It Out

Mental visualization of your objectives holds great importance in the clarity of what you intend to do along the way and what you desire as an end result. Seeing what you intend to do and what you desire and plan as if it is real is a complex mental exercise, but vital to the codification and building of the objective so as to assist the manifestation of the result. Seeing *exactly* what you desire and intend causes you to specify your wants and desires. The stronger and longer you can hold your ideal in your mind's eye, the better.

Attention Focus

Pointing your mental faculties toward the individual actions required to achieve a task, project, or goal is what causes effectiveness, as long as your acts are efficient. Continuous and persistent thinking and action toward your work, goal, project, or desired outcome can funnel or intensify the energy in a specific direction.

Efficiently and Effectively

Completion and closure of acts and tasks one-by-one in a successful manner is what creates momentum toward an objective with no need to go backward.

Presence, Awareness, Doing

Thinking and planning are most crucial. However, boldness and action are what may cause events to happen and people to be attracted to you. Therefore, contemplation mixed with action is the optimal, blended solution.

Cause/Effect: "Like Attracts Like"

Every action has a reaction. Types of actions and thoughts attract similar actions and thoughts. Kindness tends to bring kindness.

Respect tends to bring respect. Additionally, constructive thinking tends to bring constructive opportunities and events to the individual.

Increase

All mankind tends to be attracted to those who can bring them more life or enrichment. If an individual projects life and opportunity, then he or she will attract similar minds.

Insight and Restraint

Insight and restraint contain the ability to think something over, discuss it with others, or seek out counsel from others who understand or know the subject well without acting hastily. Thus, the opinion of experts and consequences are a valid consideration in thinking and acting.

Love, Forgiveness, Harmony, Dissipating Discouragement

Cultivating love and forgiveness can dispel otherwise destructive thoughts. Great minds can look back on things they love or loved, and re-harness that emotion.

Minding Your Own Business

There is something very real in taking care of yourself and your affairs. As such, your enhanced mind, body, soul, and financial affairs allow you to help those whom you love and serve humanity in better ways. The best way to be of service to humanity and your loved ones is to make the best of yourself.

Gratitude, Enthusiasm, Faith

A sincere heartfelt gratitude for life and its gifts will allow the flow of good to you. Systematic recognition of people or things to be thankful for along with gratitude may facilitate an expectation of good and growth of inherent faith. Integrating this confident expectation with your aspirations creates great power.

Guarded Speech, Response/Ability

Speaking of only positive things can attract opportunity and friends. Keeping your desires and goals close to you will keep them from becoming dissipated energy. Sharing your desires and goals with those who support, encourage, and assist you can be a positive exercise and help harvest constructive feedback.

Change/Insanity

Not evolving while continuing to do things that are failures or destructive actions tends to prevent any growth.

Creating Versus Competing

It seems that many people feel that competition causes a limited supply. However, from a supply or abundance standpoint, individuals can create without competing, to serve humanity. As an example, an individual who creates a new cure to solve a common health problem is not competing against the world, but helping it.

Right Livelihood and Labor of Love

Having a labor of love can cause effectiveness and efficiency through energetic work. Doing something that you believe in or selling a product that you have faith in, can make your job much easier or even fun. Having fun with work is a divine right.

Blessing, Praise, Protection, and Expansion

Persons who engage in a metaphysical approach seem to enjoy a greater state of well-being and success when they bless their relationship with the Universe, bless their loved ones, bless their home, and give thanks for their health on a daily basis.

Gratitude, Religion and Great Thinkers

If the only prayer you say in your life is "Thank you," that would suffice. --**Meister Eckhart**

Take full account of the excellencies which you possess, and in gratitude remember how you would hanker after them, if you had them not. --**Marcus Aurelius**

Unfolding Detachment Protected for Higher Good

When we become too attached or dependent on an external person, place, thing, or result, we can become disappointed with other people and things. It is good to expect the best, but it is also smart to allow for something better to unfold. Thus, trying to control a specific outcome without any flexibility can inhibit the Universe from its creativity.

Receiving, Valuing, Deserving

Many people from around the world feel unworthy of abundance. Many people do not value themselves, their service, their talents, and work. It is very important to learn to feel worthy, unique, and deserving of good. Moreover, you should become mentally open to receiving all good in life. Further, people should be careful to create ways to receive the good into their lives from the Universe and from others. Example: Accepting a compliment from another person.

Other People and When They Are Sent to Help You

When you engage a mentality of abundance and harmonious Spiritual thinking, your mind will expand and increase while radiating love, abundance, and health. Thus, your powers of attraction will increase. The Universe will send people to help you. It will be your job to select and allow them to assist you in a win-win relationship to expand your abundance where all can achieve a richer and fuller life through these joint ventures.

Resistance and Flow

Types of resistance that inhibit your abundance, health, and connection with Spirit are: resentment, jealousy, anger, judgment, criticism, hatred, greed, pride, and mental laziness. Other subtle resistance is to institutions, conformity, and adapting. It is better to adapt than to perish, while maintaining your unique qualities

Willingness

Willingness is the key to advancement. Be willing to take action, take a chance, or risk failure or embarrassment. Without willingness, you may never engage mental, Spiritual, or physical action that leads to good. Willingness is a vital ingredient toward successful visualization, belief, action, planning, and success. Am I willing to believe, to try, to risk, to engage? Can it be done? And why not?

Hoarding and Change

Holding onto old ideas, old things, and old ways can keep you from growth, Spiritual flow, and expansion. Taking an inventory of mental ideas and material things must be done. Eliminating the ideas, things, people, and actions that create inconvenience, frustration, clutter, and resentment will allow freedom and harmony in your life.

Recognition of Cause

It can be a fundamental mistake if you give yourself too much credit for anything good that you receive from life. Additionally, it can be a disastrous mistake to continue to blame God and the Universe for anything bad that you receive from life.

Sanity, Root Out Cause, Unlimited Potential

Root out the cause of your failures, your inconveniences, your frustration, and your mental or Spiritual disabilities. If you have a problem, there may be a cause. If you injured yourself engaging in a specific activity, you may avoid this activity in the future or better prepare for it next time. Otherwise, you may pay for this repeated action in the form of more pain and suffering. If you have a relationship that always seems to leave you in pain, then you may need to avoid this person if you are spiritually whole and the other person is not.

Giving Without Expectation, Tithing

Taking time to give money, service, or goods to divine recipients will create an untold flow in your life. Life requires circulation of your ideas, your things, and your service to humanity. With this giving, it is virtually guaranteed that your life will be blessed and protected through your giving of yourself. You are not doing this to take advantage of the law. You do this to expand your Spiritual existence, keep the flow, and give back. Expecting something in return is not needed because the Universe will provide opportunity for you by your embracing this process.

Wasting Energy and Thought

If you become frustrated every time you watch the news or read the newspaper, then why would you continue to read a specific article or watch that particular channel? It is vitally important for you to engage relaxing or strengthening activities rather than getting the same shot of bad medicine each day.

Good Deeds and Action / Balance Karma

You may feel you have wronged many people. You may even feel guilty for past deeds or encounters. However, if you feel remorse and intend to act as a better person for now on, then you have made progress. In any event, your day-to-day action and character of goodness and kindness will build your positive energy where the world has decided to protect you and serve you.

Meek Defined: Open Mind, Faith in Universe, Will of God, Spirit Before Ego

Meek is not weak. It is strong, confident, cooperative, and advantageous. Developing an honest appraisal of yourself can be healthy. You can always improve yourself, your credentials, your relationships and your business. Putting your ego first can be dangerous. When somebody has hurt your feelings, said you are wrong, said "no" to you, or otherwise attacked you, it is best to analyze (when possible) and discuss the issue with another supportive person before retaliating with e-mail, phone, letter, or in person.

Peace and Serenity Are Needed for Concentration

Peace allows growth. Clarity and concentration are primary keys to serenity. Being able to operate on a plane with singleness of mind can allow you to achieve great things. A person who cannot focus and achieve one thing at a time may never cross "the finish line" with any dream, goal, or aspiration. Overall, if you allow resentment, frustration, hate of another, or fear to dominate your thoughts, then your effectiveness will be diminished. Hard work is required to keep you focused and concentrating on bettering yourself. Overall, your freedom, vitality and wholeness depend on your effectiveness.

Visualizing Completed Transaction With Joy

We have mentioned visualization. Do not forget that you should visualize things and plans as you would have them. You should believe that they are yours in mind. Paint your ideal outcome on the mental screen in your mind's eye. Believe that it is completed. Fuse your image with love and gratitude. Celebrate its reception in your mind. Believe that you have the proper channels to receive what is coming to you. Send your vision and petition into the Universe and repeat the exercise for fantastic results.

Treasure Map and Wheel of Fortune

If you cannot paint the mental picture as clearly as you would want, then try to use the material world to enhance your mind. Cut out pictures of the ideal things you want. Put them into a collage or on poster board. Rip out images of the home you desire, people having fun, distant places that you want to visit, or the lifestyle and types of relationships that you desire. This action can help you amalgamate the images to imprint them on your subconscious mind. View them daily and place them in a prominent place. Overall, imagine having these things in your quite time. Sense the joy of receiving all of it fully.

Attraction by Thoughts

As for attraction, this can be of mind, action, and omission. You can think of something all day and possibly attract this. Further, you may act a certain way and either become it or attract it in your life. Moreover, your omissions of conduct may prevent you from steering into the direction of your life dreams.

When you consider your close family relationships, you may want to reevaluate how you respond to family members' mistakes, ideas, and thoughts. If you respond in a dubious fashion, your family members may not want to tell you about themselves. If your conversations are always woeful and negative, then your family members may consider you a toxic person. As such, if you are predisposed to being negative and a contrarian, you would probably attract others who seek to discuss the same theme with you or even try to better you in the experience of misery and misfortune. Also, your omissions are important also. If you refuse to help anyone, you may not be helped when you need it. If you omit tolerance and love to others, you may not receive it either. Thus, there is a delicate balance of give and take in the world. It is better to give now and then you shall be given to and provided for as time goes on.

With all of this in mind, it is far more practical to look at the possibilities of success, good ideas, magic, miracles, and more in others. See the God and genius in all of those you love and around you, and maybe it will be revealed and vitalized to and within you.

Chapter 7: Summary of Spiritual Empowerment

The Steps to Obtain Freedom, Peace, and Wealth

1. As beings that desire increasing life, we each contain energies of body, mind, and spirit, of which we must maintain equilibrium between all three energies. To preserve this balance we utilize our threefold powers. Use of mental, spiritual, and physical powers in a spiritual way must produce abundance.
2. All thoughts begin with an idea, which is the byproduct of divine connection to the source of all thought.
3. The ideas in back of the thought are the mystical form of all creation and the underpinnings of tangible results or manifestation.
4. All thoughts tend to lead to the field of potential outcomes for all actions, inactions, and creation.
5. Deep thinking or what is believed in mind habitually becomes who you are and is your essence or character.
6. Free will creates choices for which commitments must be selected. We all have the ability to choose how we use our free will in terms of thoughts and actions.
7. Choices create the nucleus of new form and begin a chain reaction if the choice is fueled with emotion and belief.
8. Emotions that fuel manifestation are love, joy, peace, happiness, goodness, and other positive emotions.
9. When each idea is transformed into an intention, then each intention may be transformed into a plan, vision, and mission. Then it is chosen as a prime objective for the individual.
10.   When the plan becomes your dominant thinking, it becomes a purpose that is backed by belief.
11.   When firm belief, earnestness, and constructive emotion back up a purpose, it is energized.

12.   Our belief system must be based on the constant and creative possibility of optimal results and prosperity. Everyone

who is living upright in a spiritual way is deserving and capable of tapping into this abundance.

13. We become best at co-creating our destiny when we are in spiritual unity with the universe, in which a person develops the realization of the Divine Presence within one's own self.

14. We operate most effectively when we are awakened and clear in mind. Attunement and forgiveness of ourselves and others allows us to be free of anger and to live in the present moment fully in an awakened state of mind.

15. Acceptance - We must believe that prosperity and wellbeing is our birthright.

16. Believe that you have wealth and freedom and that you are the essence of creative ability.

17. Everything that is needed is continually provided by an ever-expanding world and universe that is abundant and impersonal.

18. We must understand the essence or rationale behind the purpose of each desire that we want to cultivate.

19. Further, we must comprehend in some way how our big ideas will help others along with ourselves to convey the sincere impression of value, worth, and increase.

20. Before implementing each plan or taking any big step, we evaluate our mental effectiveness, getting clear and going thought a catharsis of mind. This means looking at your track record, atone, prune, purge, and clear away the mental debris. Begin to use "what works" and start to utilize the best practices that make you efficient.

21. Clear Objectives - Set specific goals, then research and refine them. After the purpose, task, and objective are clear, then push forward with persistence.

22. Results Driven - What is the mission, destination, vision? Develop affirmations that correlate to the most favorable end result.

23.	Think, feel, and act "AS IF" you are already in possession of the life that you want. Cultivate your emotions and your character around the "As If." You must become what you want, which means you become the person who owns the life you desire.

24.	Look at where you are and where you are going and periodically reset the course and navigation to optimize the journey.

25.	Learn to think and speak in a prosperous way that conveys peace, abundance, and increase. Mold the habits and tendencies of your thought. Refuse to accept lack and fear.

26.	Take action. Keep lists and do three things toward your dreams per day, and do them constructively to the best of your ability.

27.	Study your life, reflect on your day, and decide how to continually improve yourself. Do your homework and do all you can to learn and know your purpose, your objectives, and how to master your skills. Be the best at what you do and BE KNOWN for your excellence.

28.	Meditations and Prayer - Write out affirmative meditations such as, "Each day I am improving." Write out 10 statements that are affirming and positive. Contemplate over them each day. You can write out generalized affirmations or very specific ones.

29.	Use the affirmative statements or contemplation to increase acceptance of your potential and boost your awareness.

30.	Visualize - See yourself in optimal circumstances in your mind's eye and then feel it. If you can visualize the optimal result, then see the next step. Example: see yourself a few pounds leaner toward your optimal weight.

31.	Choose your environment. Select what to feed yourself. Mold your circumstances by your actions and specific thought.

32.   Organize your affairs. Gain the habit of finishing things well. Become excellent, simplify your life, empty the clutter, and redefine your focus. Develop prosperity-based routines.

33.   Imprint and affirm your ideals and dreams into your consciousness. The plan, desired thing, or result must be written down and then verbalized. It should be claimed into this world using the spoken word.

34.   Make wealth and excellence a priority. Align your thoughts to attract excellence and wealth. Be aware, be open, learn to receive from others, offer praise, and appreciate life. Accept your potentiality, gifts, and abundance.

35.   Circulate your GOOD. Service and Giving: donate time or money to people or organizations that are the source of your spiritual sustenance.

36.   Sixth Sense - Learn and practice creativity, awareness, and contemplation. Keep a journal, write out ideas, develop and allow a universal flow of inspiration and ideas into your life.

37.   Review and remember your actions. Reflect on what you have done well each day and the things in which you may not have excelled. Be determined to be better and do the right thing. Over 200 years ago, Ben Franklin worked his precepts of order each evening. He wanted to be excellent and build his character even at a mature age.

38.   Research ideas - what are your passions, how do your ideas serve? Listen to your intuition and cultivate strategy. Look at what it would take to implement or be successful with your new ideas, then act on them, implement the plan, review the plan, and then improve it.

39.   List streams of income and potential ways to serve and be prosperous. List how you will expand your life. Go past your comfort zones. List goals beyond your expectations and have deadlines of specificity. You can always change the date.

40.   Review your lists and projects. Check off your accomplishments.

41.   Meet with partners, family and/or spouse to define goals.

42.   Discover your natural expression. What is your labor of love? Where do your passions lie? Remember that you work to pay bills, but you should always follow your dreams. Devote 20 percent of your waking hours each week to your passion. If you become great at it, odds are you can earn a living doing it too.

43.   Character - How do you want to BE? Self-respect and self-regard can be developed and nurtured. When you rebuild yourself, you will in turn love yourself better, which allows you to be kinder, more generous, and more loving to others.

44.   With character comes responsibility toward your mental, physical, and spiritual health. Do what works to take care of yourself with diet, exercise, learning, sleep, study, and fellowship.

45.   Associate with those who can help you where you can also help them. Create a network of business and spiritual friends.

46.   Be good to yourself. Learn health self-regard and cultivate a loving relationship with the Source.

47.   Teaching others - Giving it away to keep it.

48.   Law of Increase and Charisma - Radiate abundance, cheer, and enthusiasm. Be contagious with love, cheer, and enthusiasm.

Chapter 8 - Shangri La – Secrets to Success

In this small chapter, we will divulge some of the greatest secrets to wealth and success ever known. Many people wonder why two people can be given the same recipe for happiness and one gets rich and the other fails. By reading this booklet, you will be provided the power to follow your destiny. You will also be given the steps to success and the missing secrets to happiness that are utilized by the chosen few.

Results Will Prove You Right – Analyze, Diagnose and Clarify

We are herein focused on results and results ONLY. If the system works, then there is no refuting its POWER.

Half measures will avail you nothing. You must not be a wishful person but rather a focused person filled with belief. Rather than sitting around thinking about what you would do if you won the lottery, maybe there is another way. Maybe the people that are relatively wealthy and happy are doing something different to achieve these coveted results?

Would you like a change? Do you want improvement? Are you willing to train your mind to new successful habits and character?

If you are ready, then there is a science to success and a clear and concise path to wealth, health and prosperity. All of us are using only a FRACTION of our abilities. Each one of us is a powerhouse of energy, consciousness, ideas and action.

From Pythagoras to Plato, from Spinoza to Hegel, and from Schopenhauer to Einstein, the great thinkers of all time imply the same thing. They claim that there are unseen cosmic forces that we can tap into that can energize and guide us to ideas, inventions, power and greatness.

Many of us want things but have we really been sincere? To achieve, we must be truly earnest about our goals. We must have that burning desire, which is something that you will go after and NEVER look back. This is a feeling of authentic PURPOSE where you will dedicate your whole heart to your betterment and becoming your best.

To make this big advancement, you must be willing to let go of your preconceptions. Give up your old ways and become open to a new path, new power and new abundance. What would you do if you could not fail? Truly ask yourself and petition your subconscious for inspiration and guidance. Ask for ideas, ask for help and ask for some sign that will lead you to new heights.

If you are willing to make this quantum leap, get out of your comfort zone and then learn a guaranteed method to riches and success if you are willing to put it to use with PERSISTENCE.

Unlimited Power is Yours

You have within you the power to connect to the universal force. This force is the creative and animating energy that permeates the universe. Like gravity or electricity, the Force is not seen, but exists as the all-pervading framework for which every law hinges upon. This interstellar force is also known as God or "The Life Force". This unlimited power is everywhere as creation is constant. New ideas, new art & music, new planets, new galaxies, new species, new worlds are continuously manifesting at this very moment.

That part of your mind that can be in-tune with this force is referred to by the great teachers of metaphysics as the subjective mind or higher consciousness.   Directed thought-energy can be focused where the individual may act as a creative force within the universal framework.   This supernatural power is willing to serve you and grant you anything that you earnestly and sincerely desire with focus, action, heartfelt gratitude and emotion. If Faith is the substance of things hoped for, then that very Substance can also be qualified as the energy of our attention and thoughts.   Belief and faith are the same in that they mean that we accept what is unseen. Energy is consciousness, and thus, "thought awareness" is energy. All things created equally in perfect balance, the energy of faith, attention, and mind can tilt the cosmic balance of life, happiness, and success in our favor.

This is why spiritual-metaphysics is so important because the participant who engages mental-cooperation with universal law attains the ability to optimize: body, mind and spirit. The galactic framework of forces that we seek to cooperate with is what many call: "the Spirit of the Universe" and "the spirit within you". All of us go through life with a steady stream of ideas, thoughts, and desires. Tapping into that greater, infinite-self expands our intuitive abilities to best use our priceless inspiration.   Thus, becoming aware that we may operate at a higher order of being is where achievement truly begins, and then, we become willing to take the actions that provide results. Co-operation with the "force of the universe" and the framework of the metaphysical laws that affect mankind is the path to maximize our existence, contributions, and consciousness.   Learning to use the mind and concentrate on our desires is where self actualization begins. Even the great Marconi was referred to the insane-asylum by government officials for suggesting that information and thoughts can be sent over the airwaves.   However, today all of us know that we can tune into any given channel and send messages millions of miles.   Harnessing the power of prayer, meditation and contemplation is where inspiration and well-being is cultivated. With this power of mental focus and cooperation with the universal law, we become masters of our destiny.

The Master Key List – The Plan

Begin your new life today. Write out 5, 10 or even 50 things that you want to do to improve your life and circumstances. Don't be shy! Write the amazing and exciting things you will achieve about money, travel, relationships, health or whatever. Do it and do it today. As the great poet von Goethe once implied, Begin it TODAY and there is MAGIC and POWER in it.

Write out your Master Key List and put it in your pocket. Think about it for a day. Then pick the 3 most important things you can do to change your life for the better and begin immediately to commit to those 3 goals.

Every day, when you are in your Alpha Relaxed State, you can read the list to yourself. Read it at night and upon awakening. Think about the completed successes. Think about the ESSENCE of your purpose and how you can help yourself, your family and others by attaining your dreams.

As part of your continual growth, you can enhance, add, expand and remove things from your Master Key List.

A Mental Agreement for Specific Success

Your plans and mental blueprint should be very specific. For example, you can write out on a piece of paper a personal commitment to yourself:

I, Joe Lee, Jr., will have a million dollar business 5 years from today. I will sell super creative solutions. I will provide the best service and value to my customers. My products and services will have outstanding benefits for everyone. I will do my best, work hard and remain persistent. I will not falter. Everybody will be happy to pay me handsomely for my services because they will feel great benefits from what I/we provide. I will gladly accept compensation and I will do what is needed to capture and utilize the funds. Sincerely, YOUR NAME HERE

Exercise: If we invoke the INNER POWER/SELF and EARNESTLY ask for [help, harmony and cooperation] , we are drawing closer to the Source. If we can meet the Source halfway, stay tuned into the POWER, and cooperate with the Life Force, our advancement will be speedy.

Exercise: Take some deep breaths ... You mental vibration is important. Can you take time to energize the way you feel about your goal? ... Think about a result that you want. Feel the joy of seeing it. Sense it. Emotionalize it. See your desired result in your mind's eye. Visualize it. Think As If it is YOURS. Think grateful thoughts for the imagined result or something better being manifested in your life. Send the wonderful loving thoughts into the world with heartfelt gratitude and knowing that the universe will bless you on your journey.

Definiteness of Purpose - Knowing what you want and dedicating yourself to it.

Be definite about your desires. On your list:

1. Specify what the desire is. Examples: to weigh the same amount as you did when you graduated from high school, run a marathon, get a promotion, or obtain a better home.

2. Identify exactly what you will do to achieve it.

3. Specify precisely when you will achieve it.

4. Determine what it will feel like to have it and what it will look like.

5. Imagine how you will use your success and envision what emotions you will have when you attain or use your desired outcome.

6. Take some concrete action to move toward your success each and every day.

7. If the desire is money, then specify the amount, what you will give in exchange for the money and how you will use or invest the money.

While you are building yourself up, associate with those who know about success. Ask encouraging people who know about what you want for help. Many will be happy to give you advice. Model yourself after the best and focus on the best as your belief system will certainly change for the better. Continue to use praise and appreciation in your life as this act of blessing all people and things expands your goodness and brings prosperity and appreciation to you.

When you accomplish any little thing toward your happiness, recognize the goodness of the universe. Be grateful for every small achievement and bless each and every good event that comes your way. Gratitude dispels doubt, keeps you connected, and prevents dissatisfaction. Continue to fix your attention on health, love, success, and good fortune. Your faith will be renewed.

Sincere and heartfelt thankfulness will create a newfound faith in your abilities and allow you to be connected to the great POWER within you.

Initiate Action - Using The Secret Methodology - Tips To Ensure Success.

1. When you want something badly, be sure to allow the universe to bestow upon you the thing you want or something better. Do NOT limit the universe with your desires as the supernatural power may want to give you even more than you seek in new and untold ways.

2. Pray and meditate only for good to happen to yourself and others and avoid negative thoughts or feelings for others or over any situation.

3. See the benefits and purpose of your desire and understand how your desire can help you, all involved, and even assist greater humanity.

4. Seize control of your Charisma and learn to direct and master your Personal Magnetism.

5. Focus on being creative and not just competitive. You can win with your goals and desires by creating new opportunities for yourself and all people.

6. Try to maintain harmlessness in your actions, speech and thinking.

7. Maintain personal responsibility for your actions and take care of your spiritual condition.

8. Give without the expectation of receiving and donate your time and talent to organizations that divinely inspire you and lift up your consciousness.

9. Give your attention to pressing needs first and then when you are stronger as a person, you can go for bigger and bigger goals.

10.   Learn all you can to make yourself ready and capable to achieve any of your stated desires. But remember to take action toward your goals NOW. Taking action can be reading a book, taking a course, calling somebody for an appointment or applying for a position.

11.   Keep your consciousness and mental attitude clear and efficient. If you have done harm to others, try to make it right and continuously maintain your wellbeing by maximizing the excellence of your character by practicing attunement and atonement.

12.   Make a decision. Without commitment and making something important, the ideal will only be a hopeful wish. Your job is to go to the next level and make your move to achieve what you want with all your heart and desire.

13.   Affirm your destiny. Speak it aloud to yourself every day. Say your positive affirmations and prayers out loud in the present tense with feeling and emotion. Speak constructively and learn to speak in an optimistic and confident way.

Remember, one of the greatest abilities of mankind is to give love. We live for the advancement of body, mind and soul and there is no reason to limit our capacities. Many ignorant people see wealth as greed. Ironically, poverty can and will frustrate your relationships with the spirit, other people and those you love. Accordingly, giving is one of the highest forms of love. Give yourself everything you need to become an asset to your community and to the world where one day you may give back as much as you can in great measure.

The Steps to Success – Moving Toward Your Destiny

1.   Remember that growth, prosperity and the ability to innovate, create and adapt is your birthright. You are born to be prosperous and excellent.

2.   Desire is a power seeking expression. You cannot desire what is not potentially within you; and therefore, you can be what you want to be.

3.   Desire is the result of feeling, and the feeling that results from a burning desire is a supernatural faculty seeking and demanding greater expression.

4.   Use your free time to hone your skills, improve your knowledge and prepare for your dreams and goals. Do not wait for the perfect opportunity to be all that you want to be. Become all that you can be today, and when an opportunity to be more is offered to you, be ready to take it.

5.   Use your place or present business and environment as the means to get a better one. Spend nights and weekends cultivating your abilities and preparing for greater things and the fulfillment of your goals.

6.   Everything that touches your life is an opportunity if you discover its proper use. Be aware of each circumstance and study them all for they are your opportunities. Most men fail by hoping for some particular kind of luck, instead of being ready to seize opportunities.

7.   Steadily hold the picture of all that you want to attain in person, property and environment. Form a clear conception of it. Then understand that in so far as your desires are not contrary to Eternal Justice, it is absolutely certain that you can be what you want to be. Dwell upon your goal and ideal until it is clear and definite to you and hold it until it arouses intense desire.

8.   Your vision of the right idea, if held with faith and purpose, will cause the Supreme Intelligence to move the right opportunity

toward you. Then your action, if performed with effectiveness and efficiency, will cause you to move toward the success.

9.	Pray with unfaltering grateful faith to the Supreme Intelligence that your desires shall come to you and be thankful in every prayer, petition or affirmation. Express thanksgiving with a heart full of gratitude that your desires are coming to you.

10.	Think about this ideal picture until you are always conscious of it and become in conscious possession of it with positive emotion. Presume it is yours mentally.

11.	Desire for everybody what you want for yourself. Be sure to take nothing from anybody without giving a full equivalent in life and value; the more you give, the better for you.

12.	Use each day to the fullest and do each act efficiently and effectively without haste. You must put the expanding thought into everything you do and communicate excellence to all whom you deal with.

13.	Know that others from around the world desire to help you now that you are on the supernatural path. You are to cooperate and be willing to receive this mutually beneficial exchange and assistance from those who are sent to you.

14.	The basic element of success is therefore to hold the thought and the mental attitude of advancement and to be excellent in all that you do.

15.	Strive to maintain a Consciousness of your being at one with the Spiritual Power of the Universe. Know that you are connected to the Creative Power and begin now to co-create your destiny. Utilize these steps in all of your affairs.

So the question is this: how do you become great? How do you become wealthy? How do you become successful? And, after years of research we find that most great teachers will give you the quantum mechanics of success such as: If you do certain things, you'll get certain outcomes. If you model yourself after the best, you'll get the highest rewards. If you perform the technicalities or the practical motions to attain certain consequences, you will become what you want to become. Therefore, if you go to the gym and do various and specific exercises every day results will unfold. Then, at the end of several months you'll have an optimal body, according to what you have desired or what you have planned. The real question of the day is that many people are discouraged because they don't see the results of their work in the short term or, once they feel a little better, they quit the new regimen. But remember, just like going to the gym, whether it's a mental gymnasium or the physical gymnasium, if you go to the gym and you're working out every day, at the end of 30 days, you have probably made great advances, but your body is still in transformation. Other people may notice that you've made great changes, but you may not notice yet, and that's often how these transformations occur. It is one day at a time. It's one action at a time. It's one task at a time. With focus, we can improve just about any facet of our lives. By taking these steps,, each of us will make the best of ourselves on the level of body, mind, and spirit.

This guide can create that shift and awakening that you have wanted to achieve for years. Act now and obtain the secrets for success. Keep this book close, study it and become a master of your destiny.

Chapter 9 - Conclusion: Shangri La Warrior 12 Steps to Fulfillment – Attributes of enlightened individuals

1. **Spiritual Mind** - People who live in abundance mentally, are those who put their spiritual consciousness before their ego mind. People that are able to do this tend to live more authentically and more effectively because; the mind is not clouding or limiting their cognitive abilities. These people are successful because they understand that growth is an inside job and if they can improve themselves, all will benefit.

2. **Knowingness** - Knowing that the world is an abundant place is also an empowering vibration. Those who focus on the truth of abundance, the truth of opportunity, and the facts related to an abundant world tend to believe in unlimited opportunities.   This belief energizes people to never quit, persist and seek more from life. People who engage knowingness effectively use constructive-aspiration. They know that they have choices and power over their decisions and the way that they think.

3. **Contemplative Action** - We should detach from any concepts of limitation or unworthiness and get into action. People that are engaged in constructive activities, are taking steps each day towards their goals and tend to be people who follow their dreams and complete big ideas. Life's successes are generally one step at a time, one day at a time. As such, people who finish big things are usually beginning with boldness and crossing the finish line consistently.

4. **Righteous Speech** - Use words constructively during your daily life & attempt at all times to speak and think in ways

that are related to progress, opportunity and potential. We
should speak in relation to absolute possibility.

5. **Be Excellence & Do Excellence** -   We must do each act in a
superior way and in an excellent way. We have to BECOME
the best person you can be and BECOME what we desire. Be
GREAT TO YOURSELF.   This concept is focused on self-
regard, but we also want to cultivate personal regard for
everything around us and develop a harmonious relationship
with ourselves, our neighbors, and with the universe.

6. **Co Creation and Ideas** – All of us want to find true purpose
and have a livelihood that is meaningful. If we are in
cooperation with the world and universe, this harmony will
allow inspiration which leads to ideas and creativity. It is
important to be consciously aware of the beneficence of the
universe and act on ideas that are creative and productive.

7. **Flow** - Circulate your good and empower others. This power
begins with helping others find the best in themselves, or
circulating your good.   Giving of ourselves, giving away your
services, teaching, donating excess items, teaching, or giving
to organizations and people who divinely inspire us. The
moral of the story is if we hoard our good and our stuff, it can
shut down the generous transfer of insights and business from
others.

8. **Detachment and Acceptance** – For many of us we must learn
to accept the way many things are but also accept the
opportunities and blessings. Many of us have great hopes or
ideas for our lives; however, some people are not comfortable
accepting success and greatness. If we can develop a
worthiness of our ideal outcomes in mind, the possibilities are
increased. It us up to us to cultivate a detached acceptance
and consciousness of what we want to be and have. By doing

so, the mental equivalent is produced to allow for the manifestation of our desires. Clarity is needed and detachment from the worlds follies will allow us to have the awareness and mindset to receive the good that desires to come to us.

9. **Mind Your Business** - Invest in yourself and other people. Every one of us comes to the point where we are deciding how to allocate our resources, how to allocate our time, and our energy, and our money, and many of us who have become very very successful, are those who have figured out ways to focus on investing in ourselves, becoming better people, learning new skills, learning what is going on in society and humanity, and learning how to maximize our contribution to the world and operating in a way that is a labor of love. And those who are doing these things, in this way, are the ones that are living out their true purpose and living authentically as they have the type of positive-occupational-therapy that benefits themselves and other people and as a byproduct of that activity, they are rewarded handsomely.

10.   **Give Increase to All** - What does increase mean? It means in all that you do, whether it is in your personal life or your business life, you give more than is expected of you. Give quality service and value to all people that you interact with. In this way, people will respect everything that you do because you are providing excellence and you are providing augmentation in the lives of others. Let's just say for example, you're continually providing people with better methods or better products or services which makes their lives easier. You are providing solutions, and when you provide solutions that make other people's lives better and easier. When expansion is given, you are benefited and humanity is benefits as well.

11.   **Character Expansion** - Thinking, action, and omission. How do these concepts interrelate? In essence, you character

is YOU. Thus, you are what you think, you are what do, &
you are what you do not do. The totality of your actions and
inactions becomes your character. And what that means is, if
you focus on cultivating a character that is at a higher level,
you will create a world view that is at a higher level. And so
the greater your spiritual condition—the greater your world
view. Thus, the greater your world view, the greater will be
your journey and experience. Your character defines your view
or your perception, and your perception defines your
experience, it is all tied together. And the better you take care
of your thinking and your actions and your contributions to
the world, the better your opportunity for prosperity and
excellence will be.

12.   **Bless Your World** – Bless other people, bless yourself,
seek a state of love and gratitude. Gratitude is not only is it
being thankful for what you have and having a thankful mind
and thankful heart, but it is also cultivating a grateful mind
and a grateful attitude where we are being appreciative of:
ourselves, our attributes, who we are and what we have. It
also appreciating other people and being thankful for other
individuals, places and things. This secret involves having
that harmonious, appreciative, and grateful attitude towards
our surroundings. Claim your divine abundance by having a
mindset of fulfillment and growth. Knowing that you have
enough in your life and that you're complete and whole, is one
of the keys to living in harmony and living in gratitude.   Each
day is another opportunity for change, growth, innovation and
unique expression. Overall, be on the lookout for the signs and
miracles of the universe.

Lastly, learn to be a powerful ray of sunshine to those around you.
Radiate peace and empowerment. As they say, the more you bless
other people around you in mind and deed, the odds are in your
favor that they will want the best for you as well.

Chapter 10 – Shangri-la Warrior Greatness, Health and Gratitude

The Shangri La Philosophy of Greatness

We are made of the one intelligent substance, and therefore all contain the same essential powers and possibilities. Greatness is equally inherent each unique individual, and may be manifested by all. Every person may become great. Many of the highest constituents of the Supreme Intelligence are also the constituents of man. We must learn to tap into these unused and latent spiritual powers.

We may overcome both heredity and circumstances by exercising the inherent creative power of the soul. If we are to become great, the soul must act, and must rule the mind and the body over the simple ego thoughts. Our knowledge is limited, and we fall into error through spiritual ignorance. To avoid this illusion and unawareness, we must connect our soul with Universal Spirit. Universal Spirit is the intelligent substance from which all things come. It is in and through all things. All things are known to this universal mind, and we can so unite ourselves with it as to enter into spirit and higher knowledge. To do this we must cast out of ourselves everything that separates us from the Supreme. We must have sheer willingness to live the divine and abundant life, and we must rise above all simple, trivial, & moral temptations. The seeker of spiritual abundance must forsake, repudiate, or transcend every course of action that is not in accord with our highest ideals. We must reach the right viewpoint, recognizing that God is all, in all, and that there is nothing wrong. We must see that nature, society, government, and industry are perfect in their present stage, and advancing toward completion; and that all men and women everywhere are good and perfect while each on their own journey. We must know that all is right with OUR world, and unite with the Supreme for the engagement of perfect expression & work. It is only as we see the Universal Spirit as the Great Advancing Presence in all and see the good in all, that we can shift our consciousness to real greatness.

The seeker must consecrate themselves to the service of the highest that is within, obeying the voice of their heart and spirit. There is an Inner Light in everyone that continuously impels us toward the highest, and we must be guided by this light if we would become great. We must recognize the fact that we are one with the Supreme, and consciously affirm this unity for ourselves and for all others. We must know ourselves to be a "child of God" among "children of God", and act accordingly. We must have absolute faith in our own perceptions of truth, and begin at home to act upon these perceptions.   As we see the true and right course in small things and actions, we must take that course. We must cease to act unthinkingly, and begin to think; and we must be sincere and honest in our thought. We must form a mental conception of ourselves at the highest, and hold this conception until it is our habitual thought-form of ourselves. This thought-form we must keep continuously in view. We must outwardly realize and express that thought-form in our actions. We must do everything that we do in a great way. In dealing with our family, neighbors, acquaintances, and friends, we must make every act an expression of our ideals or highest good.   The person who reaches the right viewpoint and makes this full consecration, and who fully idealizes their self as great, and who makes every act, however trivial, an expression of the ideal, has already attained to greatness. Everything we do will be done in a great way. We will inherently make ourselves known by our good work and thinking, and will be recognized as a personality of power. We will receive knowledge by inspiration, and will know all that we need to know. We will benefit from and receive all the wealth we form in our thoughts, and will not lack for any good thing. We will be given ability to deal with any combination of circumstances that may arise, and our growth and progress will be continuous and rapid. [i]

A Shangri La Exercise for Health.

A Spiritual exercise is a simple metaphysical methodology, not just in repeating words, but in the thinking of certain thoughts. Allowing these thoughts to permeate your being and sense and feel the thoughts will eventually allow them to become part of you. The words that we repeatedly say and hear become convictions. As Goethe says, the thoughts that we repeatedly think become habitual, and make us what we are. Moreover, Goethe implied that thoughts intertwined with character will enhance our action and boldness. The purpose in taking a mental exercise is that you may think certain thoughts repeatedly until you form a habit of thinking them, then they will be your thoughts all the time.

Taken in the right way and with an understanding of their purpose, mental and Spiritual exercises are of great value. The thoughts embodied in the following exercise are the ones you want to think. You should take the exercise once or twice daily, but you should muse over the thoughts continuously. That is, do not think them twice a day for a stated time and then forget them until it is time to take the exercise again. The exercise is to impress you with the formulation for continuous thought. Take a time when you can have from twenty minutes to half an hour secure from interruption and proceed first to make yourself physically comfortable. Rest at ease in a recliner, chair, bed, or on a couch; it is best to lie flat on your back.

If you have no other time, take the exercise on going to bed at night and before rising in the morning. First let your attention travel over your body from the crown of your head to the soles of your feet, relaxing every muscle as you go. Relax completely.

And next, get physical and other ills off your mind. Let attention pass down the spinal cord and out over the nerves to the extremities, and as you do so think to yourself: My nerves are in perfect order all over my body. They obey my will, and I have great nerve force.   Next bring your attention to the lungs and think: I am breathing deeply and quietly, and the air goes into every cell of my lungs, which are in perfect condition. My blood is purified and made clean.   Next, to the heart: My heart is beating strongly and steadily, and my circulation is perfect, even to the extremities. Next, to the digestive system: My stomach and bowels perform their work perfectly. My food is digested and assimilated and my body rebuilt and nourished. My liver, kidneys, and bladder each perform their several functions without pain or strain; I am perfectly well. My body is resting, my mind is quiet, and my soul is at peace. I have no anxiety about financial or other matters. God, who is within me, is also in all things I want, impelling the highest good toward me; all that I want is already given to me. I have no anxiety about my health, for I am perfectly well. I have no worry or fear whatever. I rise above all temptation of moral evil. I cast out all greed, selfishness, and narrow personal ambition; I do not hold envy, malice, or enmity toward any living soul. I will follow no course of action that is not in accord with my highest ideals. I am right and I will do right. [ii]

KEEPING THE HIGHEST HEALTH VIEWPOINT WITHIN AND WITHOUT

All is right with the world. It is perfect and advancing to completion. I will contemplate the facts of social, political, and industrial life only from this high viewpoint. Behold, life and the world is all very good. I will see all human beings, all my acquaintances, friends, neighbors, and the members of my own household in the same way. They are all good. Nothing is wrong with the Universe or my world; nothing can be wrong but my own personal attitude, and henceforth I keep that right. My whole trust is in the Supreme Master.

CONSECRATION OF THE HEALTH EXERCISE.

I will obey Spirit and be true to what within me is highest. I will search within for the pure idea of right and good in all things, and when I find it I will express it in my outward life. I will abandon everything I have outgrown for the best I can think. I will have the highest thoughts concerning all my relationships, and my manner, character, and action shall express these thoughts inwardly and outwardly. I will surrender my body to be ruled by my mind; I yield my mind to the dominion of my higher source, and I give my soul to the guidance of my higher power. [iii] * *Wallace Wattles (1910) Enhanced by Prof. Mentz*

Identification and Reconciliation

There is but one substance and source, and of that I am made and with it I am one. It is my Father; I proceeded forth and came from it. My Father and I are one, and my Father is greater than I, and I do

His will. I surrender myself to conscious unity with Pure Spirit; there is but one and that one is everywhere. I am one with the Eternal Consciousness.

Idealization

Form a mental picture of yourself as you want to be, and at the greatest height your imagination can picture. Dwell upon this for some little time, holding the thought: "This is what I really am; it is a picture of my own perfection and advancing to completion. I will contemplate the facts of social, political, and industrial life only from this high viewpoint. Behold, it is all very good. I will see all human beings, all my acquaintances, friends, neighbors, and the members of my own household in the same way. They are all good. Nothing is wrong with the Universe, nothing can he wrong but my own personal attitude, and henceforth I keep that right. My whole trust is in God.

Realization

I appropriate to myself the power to become what I want to be, and to do what I want to do. I exercise creative energy; all the power there is, is mine. I will arise and go forth with power and perfect confidence; I will do mighty works in the strength of the Lord, my God. I will trust and not fear, for God is with me. [iv]

• Remember that simple pains and discomforts are sometimes signals to take action to better your physical health; however, many pains are the body at work healing and regenerating itself on a cellular and molecular level.

- As a note, you may be able to work this positive person in your MIND for other people.

Philosophy of Gratitude

The whole process of mental adjustment and attunement can be summed up in one word: <u>Gratitude</u>.

First, you believe that there is one intelligent substance, from which all things proceed. Second, you believe that this substance gives you everything you desire. And third, you relate yourself to it by a feeling of deep and profound gratitude.

To convey the idea of your wants to the universe, it becomes necessary to relate yourself to the formless intelligence in a harmonious way.

To secure this harmonious relation is a matter of such primary and vital importance that I shall give some space to its discussion here and give you instructions which, if you will follow them, will be certain to bring you into perfect unity of mind with the Supreme Power, or God.

Many people who order their lives rightly in all other ways are kept in poverty by their lack of gratitude. Having received one gift from God, they cut the wires which connect them with the Supreme by failing to make acknowledgment.

It is easy to understand that the nearer we live to the source of wealth, the more wealth we shall receive, and it is easy also to understand that the soul that is always grateful lives in closer touch with God than the one which never looks to the SUPREME in thankful acknowledgment.

The more gratefully we fix our minds on the supreme when good things come to us, the more good things we will receive, and the more rapidly they will come. And the reason simply is that the mental attitude of gratitude draws the mind into closer touch with the source from which the blessings come.

If it is a new thought to you that gratitude brings your whole mind into closer harmony with the creative energies of the universe, consider it well, and you will see that it is true. The good things you have already have come to you along the line of obedience to certain laws.

Gratitude will lead your mind out along the ways by which things come, and it will keep you in close harmony with creative thought and prevent you from falling into competitive thought. Gratitude alone can keep you looking toward the all, and prevent you from falling into the error of thinking of the supply as limited — and to do that would be fatal to your hopes.

There is a law of gratitude, and it is absolutely necessary that you should observe the law if you are to get the results you seek. The law of gratitude is the natural principle that action and reaction are always equal and in opposite directions. The grateful outreaching of your mind in thankful praise to the Supreme intelligence is a liberation or expenditure of force. It cannot fail to reach that to which it addressed, and the reaction is an instantaneous movement toward you.

"Draw nigh unto God, and he will draw nigh unto you." That is a statement of psychological truth. And if your gratitude is strong and constant, the reaction in formless substance will be strong and continuous; the movement of the things you want will be always toward you. Notice the grateful attitude that Jesus took, how he always seems to be saying, "I thank thee, Father, that thou hearest me." You cannot exercise much power without gratitude, for it is gratitude that keeps you connected with power. But the value of gratitude does not consist solely in getting you more blessings in the future. Without gratitude you cannot long keep from dissatisfied thought regarding things as they are.

The moment you permit your mind to dwell with dissatisfaction upon things as they are, you begin to lose ground. You fix attention upon the common, the ordinary, the poor, the squalid, and the mean — and your mind takes the form of these things. Then you will transmit these forms or mental images to the formless. And the common, the poor, the squalid, and the mean will come to you.

To permit your mind to dwell upon the inferior is to become inferior and to surround yourself with inferior things. On the other hand, to fix your attention on the best is to surround yourself with the best, and to become the best. The creative power within us makes us into the image of that to which we give our attention. We are of thinking substance, too, and thinking substance always takes the form of that which it thinks about.

The grateful mind is constantly fixed upon the best. Therefore it tends to become the best. It takes the form or character of the best, and will receive the best. Also, faith is born of gratitude. The grateful mind continually expects good things, and expectation becomes faith. The reaction of gratitude upon one's own mind produces faith, and every outgoing wave of grateful thanksgiving increases faith. The person who has no feeling of gratitude cannot long retain a living faith, and without a living faith you cannot attain true prosperity by the creative method. It is necessary, then, to cultivate the habit of being grateful for every good thing that comes to you and to give thanks continuously. And because all things have contributed to your advancement, you should include all things in your gratitude. Do not waste a lot of time thinking or talking about the shortcomings or wrong actions of those in power. Their organization of the world has created your opportunity; all you get really comes to you because of them. Do not rage against corrupt politicians. If it were not for politicians we should fall into anarchy and your opportunity would be greatly lessened.

The Supreme Intelligence has worked a long time and very patiently to bring us up to where we are in industry and government, and he is going right on with his work. There is not the least doubt that he will do away with plutocrats, trust magnates, captains of industry, and politicians as soon as they can be spared, but in the meantime, they are all very necessary. Remember that they are all helping to arrange the lines of transmission along which your riches will come to you, and be grateful. This will bring you into harmonious relations with the good in everything, and the good in everything will move toward you. [v]

Chapter 11 – Shangri-La Spiritual & Ethical Principles from EurAsia

Vedic Hindu Philosophy and Spirituality

Hinduism contains a vast amount of spiritual knowledge. Many of the tenets of Hinduism are accepted by most Hindus, but universal acceptance is not the norm. Some of the major features of the Hindu belief system include: Dharma [ethics and duties], Samsara [The ongoing sycles of birth, life, death, and rebirth], Karma (action and later reactions], Moksha [which is liberation from Samsara], and various paths or practices called YOGAS.

Hinduism is monotheistic to the Supreme Spirit while also has some pantheistic properties of lesser gods. Hinduism is also panentheistic in that Hindus generally observe one God that interpenetrates every part of nature. Most Hindus believe tha the spirit self of every person called Atman is eternal while the spirit of each person is indistinct from the Supreme Spirit [Brahman]. The Upanishads which are part of the Hindu scriptures, state that whoever becomes fully aware of the ātman as the innermost core of one's own self, realizes their identity with Brahman and thereby reaches Moksha (liberation or freedom).

As for the laws of life, the Hindu law of Karma translates literally as action, work or deed and can be described as the "moral law of cause and effect". Many Hindus believe that each action or thought is recorded and has a lasting effect on our future or afterlife.

The ultimate goal of life, referred to as *moksha, nirvana* or *samadhi,* is understood in several different ways: as the realization of one's union with God; as realization of one's eternal relationship with God; realization of the unity of all existence; perfect unselfishness and knowledge of the Self; attainment of perfect mental peace

Hindu classic thought classifies particular lifestyles or goals for us. Kama [Sensual pleasure and enjoyment, Artha [Material Prosperity and Success, Dharma [Correct action in accordance with one's particular duty or spiritual laws, Moksha [Liberation from the cycle of suffering].

A Hindu practitioner has several methods [YOGAS] to achieve life goals or destiny: Bhakti Yoga (the path of love and devotion), Karma Yoga (the path of right action), Rāja Yoga (the path of meditation) and Jñāna Yoga (the path of wisdom).

Hindu Scripture

The Vedas are the ancient Hindu scriptures, written in Sanskrit and containing hymns, philosophy, and guidance on rituals for the priests of the Vedic religion. The Vedas may have been directly revealed to seers among the early Aryans in India, preserved by oral tradition. The four chief collections are the Rig Veda, Sama Veda, Yajur Veda, and Atharva Veda. The Bhagavad Gita bhagavad-gītā meaning "The Song of God", often referred to as the Gita, are the 700-verse Hindu scriptures that arepart of the epic Mahabharata which is one of the two major Sanskrit epics of ancient India. The other is the Rāmāyaṇa. The Mahabharata narrates the struggle between two groups of cousins in the Kurukshetra War and the fates of the Kaurava and the Pāṇḍava princes and their successors.

Hindu Success Spirituality

1)   Cause and Effect "Your actions and the reactions of the World" :You must be aware of your choices of mind and action. With each action, you should be able to ask the following question: "What are the potential consequences of this Choice?" To begin with, constructive actions will create and build opportunity and positive outcomes. View each choice with the end result in mind. Your choices allow you to mentally visualize or feel the outcome. Therefore, you can judge the circumstance or end result in your mind's eye and in your heart. With each choice there are questions. Will it bring me peace of mind? Right action is the right response or choice for any given situation or moment. Some of us can ask our body, heart, or Spiritual center if the choice is right. Does the choice allow us to feel comfortable sensations in our Spirit? The area of the center body gives tiny emotions or feelings that will help us make decisions if we ask in mind and heart so that we can feel our inner response. With our individual journey we can have times of joy and hardship resulting from any decision. We must be able to ask ourselves what we have learned from our journey or choices. Be aware of your choices with mindfulness. Then, try and make decisions, take action, and move ahead with your journey.

2)   Allow Your True Place to Appear: We must live according to providence. There are things that we are meant to do. We must dig deep into our souls to determine what our true purpose on earth is. Our being wants us to live and express our true talents and inner desires. You may have a dream to build hospitals, write poetry or create music. You may even have a calling to minister to the sick or poor. Whatever it is, be sure and express this before you leave this world. Many people find this true place in their labor. They call this a "labor of love or "right livelihood". This type of joyous work is easy and enjoyable regardless of how stressful it may be for others. This is because your purpose energizes your work and you are *having fun.*

3)   Prayer, Contemplation, Meditation, Self-Evaluation: What do we want from life? We want more happiness and an ability to fulfill desires. Most of us desire abundance and a flow of goodness into our lives. In the larger scheme of life, we want and desire health and a rich life in the physical, Spiritual, and mental realms. We want peace of mind and to nurture our Spirituality. Some believe that true success is the unfolding of our Spiritual life where oneness is attained with all.

The source is the Spirit and the process is the mind. We are Spiritual mind. With the mind, we have unlimited possibilities of creative thinking. Fear and doubt is also creative but limits possibilities because it can cause paralysis in your growth. Ego and control is also a block to Spiritual growth and connection with higher powers. Real power is pure, without fear, and fueled by love. Meditation, silence, and simply being are the first and primary ways to engage and receive pure power. Non-judgment creates peace in mind. Spiritual masters often suggest that you try and not judge others just for the day in thought, word, and deed.

Further, many authors recommend meditation for thirty minutes a day, twice a day. While doing so, listen to your inner and creative thoughts and intuition that come from silence. Many teachers suggest communing with nature and becoming aware of nature. Thus, open your eyes to creation. From an internal standpoint great teachers often reveal that all external relationships are a mirror of relationship with your inner self. Therefore, it is critical to obtain inner peace so that you are at peace with others. Mastering this will allow you to respond to others with awareness and compassion. With self-realization comes wealth. What is wealth? The essence of wealth is being blessed with life energy or the Holy Spirit, and you will know it when this occurs.

4)   The Law of Spiritual Detachment

Detachment and Non-resistance means to not resist moving ahead in harmony with the currents of life while maintaining and growing a sense of peace. Not allowing simple external things to hold you back. How do you achieve flow? Great teachers discuss many methods of relaxation or meditation. Men commune with nature at times to reflect on life, atone, or tune into the universal Spirit. Many Spiritual masters sincerely believe that giving attention to the "source of all" is vitally important.   Further, they imply that it is highly important to develop a harmonious relationship with the Universal Spirit or Force. This can be done, of course, through the cultivation of gratitude, prayer, and meditation. Moreover, through living a life of love, tolerance, and peace, our actions will bring us closer to the source of all.

Overall, people who actively engage a Spiritual life can become very efficient and effective because they are focused and have a state of well-being. Thus, the very experienced soul can do much less work to achieve the same degree of success as the average soul. When a person is in harmony and non-resistance with the world and motivated by love and joy, life will flow to him or her with powerful rewards. Overall, the body generates and expends energy. Selfishness and the desire to control others is a great waste of precious energy. Seeking validation and approval from everyone is also a big waste of energy. Becoming who you really are is a lifelong journey. In sum, doing esteemed actions will create esteem in your life. Unfolding to your highest level will be your reward.

5)   Some Elements of The Laws of Acceptance and Attraction:

- ➤ Acceptance of people, places, and things. Find the good in all. Develop gratitude for what is good in all things.
- ➤ Take responsibility for things as they are, and quit blaming external forces.
- ➤ Cultivate constructive thoughts and mental energy. Focus your thoughts on what you do want and *not* on what you do not want.
- ➤ Truly feel gratitude and allow emotions of thankfulness and constructive expectation to emerge from within.
- ➤ Feel gratitude for what you desire as if you had it already.
- ➤ See in your mind's eye what you want, send it into the Universe like a letter of thanks.
- ➤ Relinquish the need to argue with others regarding your point of view. This saves and builds energy.
- ➤ Remain open minded and willing for life to unfold in abundance.

> Keep specific goals, but release your desire to control exact outcomes, because the Universe may provide a better result than you could have possibly hoped for.

6)   Flow of Life and Love Energy: Giving and Receiving

Circulate your energy and Spiritual flow by giving. By giving, we receive. By doing more than the cosmos expects us to do, we are rewarded by the unbounded goodness of Karma. Give something to all persons such as the following: kind thoughts, compliments, affection, gifts of no real monetary value, compassion, radiations of your love, or bless them mentally. Giving should be unconditional without wild expectations of return of any favors or the like. Your harmonious and loving action towards others will be received and complimented in many ways. Mostly, your reward will be peace and joy, but most often, the fruits of flow come from other people who are not even related to the recipient of the initial gifts. After giving, you must be capable of receiving. Receive life's gifts and remain truly open to receive compliments, things, help, love, or even money.

7)   The Manifestation of Your Dreams.

Your body is part of the Universe and the Universe is an extension of your body. Both influence each other. You are connected to all through energy. Therefore, your mind and Spirit are directly linked to the world. Your consciousness allows you to effect and cooperate with the Universe. Focus your attention on what you really want from life and believe that it is possible. The quality of your focus and your intent has great power. Attention plus real burning desire allows you to forge ahead, organize plans, and complete major tasks. You must do all of this with a sense of love, thankfulness, and a desire to benefit mankind. Attention, intent, and desires should have fixity of purpose. This means to hold attention on a positive outcome. Avoid directing your attention toward your obstacles and hardships. These difficulties can be changed to opportunities if you are paying attention.

8)   Some Steps to Manifesting Your Desire:

- ➤ Go into silence.
- ➤ Focus your attention upon your dreams and objectives.
- ➤ Release your carefully chosen desires.
- ➤ Don't be influenced by others' opinions, and keep your desires to yourself.
- ➤ Cultivate gratitude toward the world and allow the universe to help you.
- ➤ Relinquish attachment or anxiety toward the exact outcome.
- ➤ Allow a higher or better outcome to come into your life.
- ➤ Make a list of your desires and read them each day and night.
- ➤ Pay attention to people, places, and things that are sent to assist you in your journey.

9)   The Laws of Release and Cooperation

Relinquish attachment and surrender your desires to the greater all. But, you should still maintain your desire, attention, and focus. Just continue to *send* the desire into the greater world with great faith, much like sending a mental telegram to the great force. Releasing allows you to continue to create and improve on your original desire as you go along. There is a big materialistic flaw in this Philosophy – "When I get the next thing, I will be happy." This type of statement can be destructive because it can become a cycle of frustration, and we may never be satisfied. Thus, work hard and allow life to unfold while not being be too controlling, i.e., be flexible. In sum, allow all of the best possibilities or alternatives, and try not to force things to happen, staying alert to the options and possibilities. When you are prepared and meet the options that life gives you, this is excellent fortune.

10) Success in the Now

There is not other time but now. Your truth is what is here but sometimes beyond what you may see. We must stay aware to opportunity and possibility today. Yesterday and tomorrow cannot be acted upon today. Seek joy and happiness now. Allow your mind to engage bliss and contentment. In this day, you can do what is necessary toward your dreams and goals. However, be your best and do what you do well. As time moves forward, your harmonious actions will add up and your character will be more than it ever was. Character is the totality of your actions, thinking, omissions, and energy. If you are building character and momentum in your mind and world, other people and the Universe will instinctively know this. Therefore, your powers of attraction and usefulness to humanity will be appreciated, valued, and utilized. With your energy in the now and your consciousness directed and pointed at *growth*, you will begin to flow effortlessly with life. Provided that you maintain a sense of peace and wholeness, you will maintain a connection to the universal power. In sum, your will can fuse and be energized by the true guidance of the world.

Mystic Persian Philosophy

Underlying Beliefs of Persian Mysticism

1. Common thread running through all religions
2. There is One God, The Eternal.
3. The primal goal of Mystics is to let go of all notions of duality, including the conception of an individual self, and to realize the Divine unity.
4. There is central truth in religious scripture
5. There is one brotherhood of man which unites all children under the fatherhood of God.
6. Love is the supreme moral principle
7. Self Understanding
8. Profession of Faith, Prayer, Fasting, Pilgrimage, and Charity.

Thoughts from "The Alchemy of Happiness" by Ghazzali - Abu Hāmed Mohammad ibn Mohammad al-Ghazzālī (1058-1111) "The first step to self-knowledge is to know that thou art composed of an outward shape, called the body, and an inward entity called the heart, or soul. By "heart" I do not mean the piece of flesh situated in the left of our bodies, but that which uses all the other faculties as its instruments and servants. In truth it does not belong to the visible world, but to the invisible, and has come into this world as a traveler visits a foreign country for the sake of merchandise, and will presently return to its native land. It is the knowledge of this entity and its attributes which is the key to the knowledge of God."

Mawlānā Jalāl-ad-Dīn Muhammad Rūmī – (1207-1273) Rumi's Poetry of Love, "Love's nationality is separate from all other religions, The lover's religion and nationality is the Beloved (God). The lover's cause is separate from all other causes, Love is the astrolabe "astrological compass" of God's mysteries.

*Both Rumi and Ghazzali were Muslim theologians, jurists, philosophers, psychologists and mystics of Persian origin.

Theosophy - Literally "God-wisdom"

The Theosophical Society was founded in New York City in 1875 by H.P. Blavatsky, Henry Steel Olcott, William Quan Judge and others. Its initial objective was the investigation, study and explanation of spiritualist and occult phenomena. After a few years Olcott and Blavatsky established the International Headquarters at Adyar, Madras, India. They soon became focused on studying Eastern religions. By 1889 when Blavatsky wrote Key to Theosophy, the Society's objectives had evolved into:

1. **To form the nucleus of a Universal Brotherhood of Humanity without distinction of race, colour, or creed.**

2. **To promote the study of Aryan and other Scriptures, of the World's religion and sciences, and to vindicate the importance of old Asiatic literature, namely, of the Brahmanical, Buddhist, and Zoroastrian philosophies.**

3. **To investigate the hidden mysteries of Nature under every aspect possible, and the psychic and spiritual powers latent in man especially. (p. 39, Key to Theosophy)**

Basic Beliefs:

- **Karma** – men to free themselves from unconsciously causing karma, which has become the cause of suffering of men during life, through an emulation of dharma-duty to all that lives
- **Reincarnation** - Theosophists believe that all human beings in their "Higher Selves" are immortal
- All life is connected whether animal, vegatabal or mineral
- **That religion, philosophy, science, the arts, commerce, and philanthropy, among other "virtues," lead people ever closer to "the Absolute."**
- Evil and good are the result of human determination, and of themselves are illusions

- Depending on what branch of Theosophy you study, it may contain a much greater component of Esoteric Christianity.

7 Levels of Theosophical Development of the Spiritual Seeker – Laws of Seven. This is also similar in Rosacrucianism.

1. Raw Form
2. A model or form (physical component)
3. The Breath of Life or Thought – Spark of Creation
4. Desire or Impelling force of Thought and Will
5. Ego thought consciousness (Needs to be refined)
6. To awaken, enlighten, know i.e. Refined Thinking
7. The seventh is called Atman (Sanskrit). Pure consciousness. It is the feeling and knowledge of "I am," pure thought and cognition/mind.

This analysis above also applies to the 7 stages of growth of man. Each of us has cycles which easily correlate to our growth, puberty, manhood/womanhood, intelligence and wisdom development.

Buddhist Eight Fold Path to Happiness

The **Noble Eightfold Path** - Essentially a practical guide of bringing about ethical and meditative discipline, the Noble Eightfold Path forms the fourth part of the Four Noble Truths, which have informed and driven much of the Buddhist tradition. Budda: Siddhartha was born in Lumbini and raised in the small kingdom or principality of Kapilvastu, both of which are in modern day Nepal. Nepal is the most Northern section of India which is between Europe and China.

4 Noble Truths: 1) The Nature of Suffering (Dukkha):

"This is the noble truth of suffering: birth is suffering, aging is suffering, illness is suffering, death is suffering; union with what is displeasing is suffering; separation from what is pleasing is suffering; not to get what one wants is suffering; in brief, the five aggregates subject to clinging are suffering."   2) **Suffering's Origin (*Samudaya*):** "This is the noble truth of the origin of suffering: it is this craving which leads to renewed existence, accompanied by delight and lust, seeking delight here and there, that is, craving for sensual pleasures, craving for existence, craving for extermination." 3) **Suffering's Cessation (*Nirodha*):** " This is the noble truth of the cessation of suffering: it is the remainderless fading away and cessation of that same craving, the giving up and relinquishing of it, freedom from it, nonreliance on it." 4) **The Way (*Marga*) Leading to the Cessation of Suffering:** This is the noble truth of the path leading to the cessation of misery which is the Noble Eightfold Path; that is, right view, right intention, right speech, right action, right livelihood, right effort, right mindfulness, right concentration.

1. Right View

This means to see, interpret, and believe the Highest Truth. It is simple to see things as misery and suffering. It is more noble to see life as a miracle and see beyond what the critical mind can see. The right view affords peace of mind, the ability to take action, and a sense of well-being. We eventually become what we think about all day; thus, our views and how we focus our attention are extremely important. Thinking bigger ideas of abundance, health, love, and so on, is a much greater force than negative ideas. Harmony leads to peace.

2. Right Intention

Intention is also similar to desire or purpose. If we are definite in our intentions and purpose, our dreams can unfold along the lines of our true path. Writing down our intentions is well enough, and has its effect, especially upon ourselves, in clarifying our vision and strengthening our faith; but it is not our oral or written petitions that get us what we want. In order to have abundance we do not need a "minute of prayer and concentration"; we need to "focus without ceasing during all hours." And by focus I mean holding steadily to your vision, with the purpose to cause idea creation into form. We can operate on a plane of mental harmony and good will, and we can flow constructively with life. It is better to not resist everything. We can allow life to unfold in conjunction with our constructive and faithful action. We can make the best of ourselves while in a state of well- being. Our highest truth is harmony, health, and success.

3. Right Speech

Guard and craft your speech carefully. Never speak of yourself, your affairs, or of anything else in a sympathy seeking or discouraging way. Never admit the possibility of failure, or speak in a way that implies disenchantment as a possibility. Never speak of life, career, or the economy as being hard, or of business conditions as being terrible. Times may be hard and business is bad for those who are operating in a Godless scramble within the competitive plane.

You are a constructive creator, your ideas help people, your ideas do not take away from anyone, you can create what you want, and you are above fear. When others are having hard times and poor business, you will find your greatest opportunities. Right speech means the way you talk to others and to yourself. Train yourself to think and speak of life getting better and better with unlimited opportunities. Always speak in terms of advancement; to do otherwise is to deny your faith.

4. Right Action

Every act is, in itself, either effective or inefficient. Every inefficient act is a failure, and if you spend your life in doing inefficient acts, your whole life may become a loss. The more things you do, the worse for you, if all your acts are inefficient ones. On the other hand, if your every action is a success in itself, and if every act of your life is an efficient one, your whole life will be a success. The cause of failure is doing too many things in an inefficient manner without focus, and not doing enough things in an effective manner. You will see that it is a self-evident proposition that if you avoid inefficient acts, and if you do a sufficient number of efficient acts, you will harvest a richer and fuller life. Every action is either strong or weak; and when every one is strong, you are acting in the right way, which allows prosperity for you and your family. Every act can be made strong by holding your vision while you are doing it, and putting the whole power of your love, faith, gratitude, attention, and purpose into it. Further, our minds should facilitate ways and means to capture, receive, and harvest what life has to offer us so that we can use it for our betterment and to help others as well. Never allow yourself to feel disappointed. You may expect to have a certain thing at a certain time, and not get it at that time; and this will appear as a loss. But if you hold to your faith, you will find that the failure is only apparent. Go on in the mindful way, and if you do not receive that thing, you will receive something so much better that you will see that the seeming loss was really a great success.

5. Right Livelihood

Right livelihood means that one should earn one's living in a Spiritual and joyous way. People should be able to follow their dreams and exercise their God-given talents in the form of livelihood. Therefore, we should be able to work and have fun while being rewarded for what we have given and produced for others. Right livelihood means creating win-win relationships and business dealings where everybody benefits while you use your divine gifts of labor. Your work is for the good of all involved and everyone receives some type of increase and advancement in their lives for interacting with you. Before you become fearful of success, realize that poverty and self-sacrifice are *not* pleasing to God. And, remember that extreme altruism is no better and no nobler than extreme selfishness; both are mistakes. You need not entertain the thought of competition. You are to create, not to compete for what is already created. You do not have to take anything away from any one. You do not have to cheat, obsessively bargain, or to take advantage in negotiations. You do not need to let any man work for you for less than he earns. You do not have to covet the property of others; no man has anything of which you cannot also achieve. You are to become a creator, not a competitor; you are going to get what you want, but in such a way that every other man will have more because of your actions.

6. Right Effort

Right effort can be seen as a prerequisite for the other principles of the path. Without effort, which is in itself an act of will, nothing can be achieved, whereas non-definite effort distracts the mind from its task, and confusion may be the consequence. Thus, you must really desire prosperous effort in your life. The more clear and definite you make your picture of your objectives, the stronger your desire will be; and the stronger your desire, the easier it will be to hold your mental energy fixed upon the picture of what you want. Behind your clear vision must be the purpose to realize it, to bring it out in tangible expression. Right efforts and work mixed with confident expectation or faith will be alive with results.

And behind this purpose must be an invincible and unwavering belief that the thing is already yours, that you already have it in your mind and you need only to take possession of it and receive it with open arms and mind. Live in the new objective, mentally, until it takes form around you physically. No haste is required. However, we know effort is reduced by preparedness. Thus, being ready in your mind, body, and Spirit can enable seamless effort and flow of action. In the mental realm, enter at once into full enjoyment of the things you want. "Whatsoever things ye ask for when ye pray, believe that ye receive them, and ye shall have them," said The Great One.

7. Right Mindfulness

Right mindfulness is the controlled and perfected faculty of cognition. It is the mental ability to see things as they are, with clear consciousness. Usually, the cognitive process begins with an impression induced by perception, or by a thought, but then it does not stay with the mere impression. *A man's way of doing things is the direct result of the way he thinks about things.* To do things in a way you want to do them, you will have to acquire the ability to think the way you want to think; this is the first step toward achieving abundance. *To think what you want to think is to think the truth, regardless of appearances.*

Every man has the natural and inherent power to think what he wants to think, but it requires far more effort to do so than it does to think the thoughts that are suggested by surrounding appearances. To think according to the environment is easy; to think truth regardless of appearances is laborious and requires the expenditure of vast energy, mental power, love, and faith. This is possible for you if you are willing to train yourself and allow yourself to grow along these lines. The more you can harmoniously focus your mind while imagining all of your goal's delightful details, the better. This will bring the Universe in harmony with your highest good, which the Universe must answer for you. Mindfulness also implies that we should be aware that others on this earth are here to help us and may offer assistance. We should be in tune with these opportunities that may come from many places in the form of other people seeking us out.

8. Right Concentration

The eighth principle of the path, concentration, is described as one-pointed-ness of mind, meaning a state where all mental faculties are unified and directed onto one particular object.

By thought, the thing you most sincerely desire is brought to you; by action you receive it. Hold concentration with faith and purpose. See the vision of yourself in the better environment. Act upon your present environment with all your heart, and with all your strength, and with all your concentration. Hold the vision of yourself with the right outcome or opportunity, with the purpose to get into it, and the faith that you will get into it, and are getting into it; but act in your present opportunity. Use your present situation or business as the means of getting a better one. Your vision of the right purpose or goal, if held with faith and purpose, will cause the Universe to move the right opportunity toward you; and your action, if performed in the light of harmonious intention and concentration, will cause you to move toward the opportunity.

See the things you want as if they were actually around you all the time; see yourself as owning and using them. Make use of them in imagination just as you will use them when they are your tangible possessions. Dwell upon your mental picture until it is clear and distinct, and then take the mental attitude of ownership toward everything in that picture. Take possession of it, in mind, in the full faith that it is actually yours. Hold to this mental ownership; do not waiver for an instant in the faith that it is real. And remember this about gratitude; be thankful for your life and desires "at all times" as you expect to be when it has taken form. The man who can sincerely thank the Universe for the things he owns only in imagination, has real faith. He will have abundance and peace; he will cause the creation of whatsoever he wants.

Summary of The Eightfold Path

Becoming a warrior at true peace with yourself is the key. Bridging your actions to your Spiritual mind and body is where focus, poise, effectiveness, and success emerge. To advance quickly, man must form a clear and definite mental image of the things he wishes to have, to do, or to become; and he must hold this mental image in his thoughts while being deeply grateful to the Universe that all his highest needs and desires are granted to him. The man who wishes to have an abundant and prosperous life must spend his leisure hours in contemplating his vision, and in earnest thanksgiving that the reality is being given to him. Too much stress cannot be laid on the importance of frequent contemplation of the mental image, coupled with unwavering faith and devout gratitude. This is the process by which the impression is given to the Universe, and the creative forces are set in motion. Your mind will then begin working with you to allow right attention, concentration, and livelihood on a level of love, harmony, faith, and gratitude. Defining your purpose in life or aiming towards specific outcomes while allowing them to unfold in higher and better ways will be where the Spiritual miracles appear. Moreover, allowing your talents, true place, and right career to become part of your life will also be part of your journey. Ultimately, intertwining your concentration, mind, speech, and view to your action will be the missing link of success.

Combining the sharpened mind with action is where your daily results begin to add up and build momentum towards growth and expansion.

*Passages compiled from several authors with insights from Prof. Mentz and   W. D. Wattles included.

Egyptian Greek or Hermetic – The Kyballion Laws

The Kybalion was first published in December of 1908 by The Three Initiates who was probably Dr. William Walker Atkinson and his associates. The book dedicated to Hermeticism and the Ancient Mystics of the Greek and Egyptian Empires. The Kybalion it states that the book was published by Yogi Publication Society which runs out of the Masonic Temple in Chicago, IL.   Some calculate that the Kybalion is an work of an older Greek manuscript called the Kabalyon from several thousand years ago.

The Kybalion speaks of 2 major issues: 1) The ALL in All and 2) Cause and Effect.

The "All in All" can be related the reasoning that we are part of ALL and the Supreme. We, of course, do not contain ALL that the Supreme is composed of. However, we are connected to ALL and contain a part of it. Therefore, we are connected to all being and universal substance. Moreover, the ALL contains all of what we are. With this in mind, it parallels many of the Ancient Eastern Mystics such as: Christians such as Meister Eckart, Budda, Vedic Teachings, Socrates,Swedenborg, and more.

Additionally, if we are part and connected to all, we can communicate to all via the Hermetic Teachings of Mentalism, Vibration, Cause and Effect and our Mind Thoughts and Actions.

With cause and effect, we know that even Plato and Aristotle realized that every effect has a cause. There is a chain of events and mind stuff that leads to every outcome. Although we may not cause every specific outcome, we play a part in each chain of causation.

With vibrations, many teachers are explaining to students how to affect their personal vibratory and rhythmic rates of thinking, moods, and even prayer and meditation. With concentration, focus, and mental imaging, we can affect our future and the energy that precedes us.

Notes on The Seven Hermetic Principles

I. THE PRINCIPLE OF MENTALISM

As we are Spirit and are part of ALL, our minds must work in tune with the infinite. Thus, we have a duty to mentally work in harmony with the spirit within and without. The closer we bring ourselves to the source of all, the closer it will draw to us. There is a connecting link between us and the ALL that we can clog up or block with the emotions of: pride, fear, or anger etc. Thus, the goal is that mind and spirit within can work in accordance with the spirit throughout and surrounding us. We must meet the All half-way with our thought and action

II. THE PRINCIPLE OF CORRESPONDENCE.

"As above, so below; as below, so above."–The Kybalion – With this statement we determine that our present and past mind function and focus corresponds with our reality. We can will our minds to focus or concentrate in any direction with which corresponding energy will meet us in the future. The Mind is the creator of the reality that we have and will have. Various influences may affect the path, but we can be in continuous contact with the universal forces which alters the journey. Realizing that the spirit energy of ALL is contained within is the breakthrough, but having a harmonious relationship with the spirit energy within and without is the key to initial & long-term prosperity.

III.   THE PRINCIPLE OF VIBRATION.

Your vibration can be at many levels. To say the least, you can enhance your mental vibration through various actions. Higher levels of mental and spiritual vibrations include: Love, Gratitude, Praise, Faith, Feel good emotions and more. Therefore, many practitioners work on a daily basis to enhance and bring their mental and spiritual vibration to a higher level. Practitioners do this so that they may lead a more harmonious life, but also to attract people, events and things of the same or higher vibration. The end result of healthy vibrations is the attraction of more constructive events, outcomes, and possibilities.

IV.   THE PRINCIPLE OF POLARITY.

All things and issues have 2 sides. As stated in this paper, cold and heat are degrees or fluctuations of the same thing such as climate. Other examples include love and dislike or truth or half-truth. There are 2 sides to everything, thus looking beyond what is apparent and searching deeper for the truth is important. Why is this important? The understanding of the poles and truths allows us to flow with the world instead of fighting events. This is because we are able to respond in a spiritual manner until we understand the event better. As an example, something may happen that is NOT a result that we wanted. However, after continuing our efforts and moving forward with action, we may find that something better is coming to us in due time. When we are in tune with the spirit and energy of all, we are able to best respond to happenings in a spiritual way. Without reacting, we maintain our composure, focus on today and continue to move forward without engaging a senseless battle. From this flow and patience, we are able to bring even higher prosperity, greater success, and peace of mind to ourselves.

V. THE PRINCIPLE OF RHYTHM.

Life and events can swing like a pendulum. A practitioner can learn to control their mind and spirit energy to keep harmony through life's ebb and flow of events, personalities and thought. As an example, you can neutralize your destructive thoughts with thoughts of: Blessing, Praise, Love, Gratitude, Acceptance, and Faith. Even in instances of envy or jealousy, we must praise our homes, spouses, children, other people of success and wealth, and friends. When we bless and mentally praise others, we neutralize any fears and jealous thoughts and therefore attract wealth, health and peace of mind in our own reality of energy.

VI.   THE PRINCIPLE OF CAUSE AND EFFECT.

For every thought, action or inaction, there is a corresponding thought and event. Your heartfelt emotions when mixed with constructive thought and action carry more force than the average thought and action. Building a foundation is vital to this step. At first, we must change our mentality to one of lack to a mind of possibility. Our minds grow and begin to believe in opportunity and abundance. Instead of doubt, we transcend to a spiritual position of why not. At this juncture, we begin to take action in accordance with our dreams. Each mental and physical action we take on a daily basis adds to the momentum of our spiritual force. Our spiritual force in conjunction with our harmonious and constructive thinking begins to manifest higher realities in our days to come.

VII. THE PRINCIPLE OF GENDER.

Each person or event may have a gender-like energy built into it. Learning what energy is at the heart of each issue or situation is very helpful. The practitioner may be able to better work with events and people if they understand the underlying energy of it. Understanding the feelings, emotions, logic, and purpose of each person, place or event can allow us to work better with it or even allow us to avoid it if necessary. The teachings herein include statements about the Conscious and Subconscious Mind and the I and Me. Thus, there is an WITHIN component to this principle. Each person must understand that their mind is like a computer but you are the operator. You must realize that what you put on your hard drive can affect your Operating System and your Memory and function. Further, if you clear your mind and spirit via exercises of prayer, affirmations, good diet, exercise, and self examination you can also improve your spiritual and mental function much like a virus software or a charged battery can clear out the junk from your computer and improve performance. Once again, in your mind is the computer and the operator of the computer.

Both have a voice. Knowing which one is speaking to you takes some effort and concentration. As a note, many people have been pre-programmed from family, friends, and exposure. This programming may have your hard drive overloaded with no room for advancement. Knowing when to clear out the hard drive and defragment the drive is important. Your intuition will speak to you if you need to work on this type of catharsis.

The Synthesis of the Ancient Greco-Egyptian Hermetic Principles

It can be said that a master of the 7 principles has become spiritually awaken from the state of illusions. When effectively working the Hermetic steps herein, the practitioner's awareness can be opened where they are in tune with the infinite.

When a person opens their eyes, mind, senses, and heart to opportunity, life, bliss, creation and love, the world can blossom before their eyes on each waking day. Instead of waking up believing in doom and gloom, the practitioner is waking up expecting the cooperation of the world, universe and spirit. While recognizing the source of the power, the adherent also manages his or her thoughts, mental vibration, spirit rhythm so as to radiate only the best energy to the source and to others operating on this physical plane.

Remember, your force and energy is yours to protect and strengthen. Don't let others tap into it and try and drain you. Via these principles, you see that your energy can be augmented, drained or tainted. Other people who do not understand your force, may carry negative energy or particles that can enter your wave or field. You understand that your mental and spiritual focus on strength, happiness, success, prosperity, health, faith and confidence will keep your field strong. However, other tainted people may carry particles that are somewhat contagious. Examples are: Complainers, Fear Mongers, and Pessimists. The only way for you to deal with these people is to convey your optimism, avoid them, or neutralize them with thoughts and feelings of love, compassion, and peace. Never bother fighting them and simply allow them to be. All is right with your world, and you need not try to change them in any drastic manner. Your action, faith, character, and prosperity will eventually gain their attention and respect.

As with probabilities, each person may have many destinations but engage only one plane of the journal at a time. Thus, actions and causes can put you on another fork of possibilities in the chain of causation. Knowing how to take action or maneuver the energies and opportunities in the external world will allow you to make positive and constructive choices on your path. As you know, faith is an expectation of something better and good on a daily basis. Faith involves confidence and resolve over your constructive beliefs. As an example, scientists say that the earth has magma at its core, but nobody has ever been to earths center. We just take it as fact. The Hermetic Master knows that pure spirit is at the core of the source of all there is based on their experience and working with the art of cooperating with the Source of ALL. In the same way, every person of intellect knows that bad germs and parasites can destroy an unhealthy host. Scientists also know that there are healthy forms of inner agents such as white blood cells or other natural immunities. Therefore, the master understands how to attract healthy agents and also to become immune to unhealthy forces by neutralizing them by entering the 4th dimension of peace, love, confidence, and prosperity.

Understanding the energy of other beings or forces, allows the master to interrelate on this earthly plane in the most effective manner without harm. The person who best employs these secrets will reach heightened awareness and keep a calm focus on their purpose using their powers effectively each day. The end result is prosperity, health, harmony, growth, and peace.

Hermes Trismegistus depicted in a medieval rendering.

Noble Virtues Nordic Philosophy – From Scandinavia to Russia

The **Noble Virtues** are the ethical code gleaned from various sources including the Poetic Edda particularly the Hávamál, the Icelandic Sagas, Germanic Warriors along with Roman and Greek SpiritualTeachings.

1. **Strength is better than weakness.**   Strength is something earned. It takes willingness and effort to obtain strength. When we intentionally grow our strength or latent powers, we are able to meet opportunities or challenges with preparedness. Weakness can be in the form of mental, physical, or spiritual weakness. Upright living and balance can prevent most instances of weakness.
2. **Perseverance** and Courage is better than cowardice. Examples of courage are acting with boldness to help others or even maintain your responsibilities.   In today's world, perserverance implies action. Taking action and not procrastinating. Without action, an idea can not even begin any movement or obtain energy that it needs to manifest.
3. **Discipline** and Joy are better than guilt. Sooner or later, we must learn when to work and when to enjoy life in its purest form.
4. **Honor** is better than dishonor. What is Honorable? Being honorable involves your thought, word and deed. A man of faith, service and charity and whose self control transcends all drama and hostility.
5. **Self Reliance** & Freedom is better than slavery. As they used to say, the sharecropping system was "Slavery by Debt." Thus, we must learn to break free of over-dependence or being tied down to anything that can cause injury over the long term. We we make the best of ourselves from a standpoint of mind, education, health, body, spirit, harmony and so forth, we become free to express ourselves naturally and effectively.

6. **Hospitality** and Kinship is better than alienation. Hospitality was a word that implied helping our brothers and sisters. The word Charity is most often used in our busy lives today. What is key to the concept of hospitality is "loving thy neighbor" as ourselves. By helping others and being of service to others, we open the door for the universe to shower us with opportunity and gifts.

7. **Truth** and Realism is better than dogmatism. What is the truth? Do we know the facts? Should we try to learn more? Do we have time to investigate? Do we need to take action? Is the meaning that we have attached to the truth destructive or constructive?

8. **Industriousness** and Vigor is better than lifelessness. As we know, doing 2 or 3 things per day effectively can add to a mountain of advantages during a lifetime. If we can help ourselves and help others, the entire family and community benefits and excels.

9. **Fidelity** is better than universalism. Being true to yourself and following your dreams leads to your happiness and everyone elses happiness also. We are all unique and qualified to be our best in whatever endeavor we can achieve. We must make decisions, we must take positions, and we must take action. Sometimes we must chose sides. With that being said, we must be strategic with our decisions while also trying to intelligently foresee the consequences of each of our individual decisions.

Tree of Life or The Nordic Yggdrassil

All living Nature is represented in the figure of the ancient Yggdrasill. The name historically means "Odin's Horse, chariot or seat." The living world is regarding as moved and guided by the divinity which has its seat therein, as the Spirit in the body. The name in this sense fully coincides with the spirit of Old-Norse poetry: and the myth of the Yggdrassil appears throughout poetic allegory. The Tree or Worlds are really a symbol of the multidimensional structure of reality. *Image Below: copyright by Mentz

As you can see, the tree of life and its' worlds shows Consciousness & Awareness (SPIRIT) at top as a higher world and Hell at the bottom listed as unconsciousness and "living in illusion". There are several worlds in-between which are indicative of our challenges and abilities to traverse through life effectively in our quest for freedom from illusion and misery.

Taoism from Ancient East Asia

The Classic Text of the ***Dao De Jing by* Lao tzu** - **Taoism, Tao or DAO**

Taoism is probably the most ancient of the Chinese Religious Philosophies possibly dating farther back than 3000 BC. The philosophy has quite an amazing undertone of tuning in with nature both externally and internally. Because Tao is consider the underlying force or spirit of everything, the use of or invoking of the word Tao has a very spiritual essence. Many writers refer to Tao much like Westerners would refer to the "power of the universe" or "the forces of nature". It can also be said that a Taoist is a Spiritual Alchemist who believes that the physical body is a one with ALL along with the internal corresponding to the external.

Taoists accepted that the Tao is all permeating, a great oneness from which all things emanate. Moreover, a Taoist generally believes in the Eastern Philosophy that each of us is a microcosm of the great ALL where the power of Yin and Yang are involved. Ying and Yang may be discusses as differences in thought such as reality and illusion or login versus emotion.   Hermetic thought may more distinguish Yin and Yang by discussing the gender related aspects of Yin and Yang such as the feminine Yin power of creativity.

With the All Permeating Force and Energy, Taoist believe that we are in an unformed and natural state. Thus, our cooperation with the Tao allows co-creation of our lives. As such, our thinking and "way of life" actually creates our world.

Also, Taoists are adherents to variations of breathing exercises which involves bringing in life energy. This is also a pathway to become more one with the ALL in breath , life, silence or thinking. Naturally, Taoists enjoy breathing exercises where the vitality of life is inhaled while exhaling the impurities of the body and mind.

Taoists lean toward natural expression. This belief coincides with flowing with life instead of fighting against it. Many say that the Taoist life involves more spontaneous and free conduct. Moreover, NeoTaoists seem to have a great focus on a stricter Authenticity in living and being true to your nature.

Also, emptiness in Taoism is something that brings us closer to Tao. For example, moving aside the racing thoughts of our daily life, becoming still & relaxed, and listening to our heart or spirit.

Because Taoism is always open to change, it is considered an optimistic philosophy. Change can also be facilitated by the practitioner by putting yourself into another's position mentally to see their perspective. Further, it may be healthy to analyze our perception of others to analyze our thinking.

Overall, expressing your true nature and talents allows the practitioner to be in tune with the TAO. Using opposing forces to your advantage is one of the key elements to the Mental and Physical TAO Philosophy. This is quite similar to the Egyptian and Greek points of the Kyballion Hermitic System. As such, Taoism is a preemptive philosophy that aspires to mitigate problems or optimize success by taking action sooner than later.

Like the Myth of the Yellow Emperor who backed off from micromanaging his people, Taoist beliefs suggest that non-interference with people can actually allow them to flower and unfold better than our expectations toward their true place or "right livelihood". This philosophical aspect of Taoism emphasizes various themes found in the *Tao Te Ching* (道德經) such as: naturalness, vitality, peace, "non-action" (*wu wei*), purity/emptiness (refinement), harmony, the strength of softness (or flexibility), and in the *Zhuangzi* 《庄子》 such as receptiveness, spontaneity, the relativism of human ways of life, ways of speaking and guiding behavior.

Taoist Core Concepts and Beliefs

1. Tao is the primal-cause of the universe. It is a force that permeates through all life.
2. **"The Tao surrounds everyone and therefore everyone must be aware to find enlightenment."** [4]
3. Each practitioner's goal is to harmonize themselves with the Tao.
4. The Taoist scholars view the many gods as manifestations of the one Dao, *"which could not be represented as an image or a particular thing."* Taoists seek solutions to life's challenges through inner meditation and outer observation.
5. Taoists strongly promote vitality through breath exercise. Each person must nurture the *Ch'i* (air, breath) that has been given to them.
6. Development of virtue is one's chief task. The *Three Jewels* of Virtue to be seek out are compassion, moderation and humility.
7. Taoists follow the art of *"wu wei,"* which is to let nature take its course.
8. One should plan in advance and be mindful of consequences
9. A Taoists extends kindness to others, in part because such an action tends to be reciprocated.
10. Taoists believe that **"people are compassionate by nature and inherently good...left to their own devices people will show compassion without expecting a reward."**
11. The 5 main organs and orifices of the body correspond to the 5 parts of the sky: water, fire, wood, metal and earth.
12. Time is cyclical, not linear as in Western thinking. i.e. cycles of life will occur.

Earliest Indo-European Religions

The most ancient world religions of Mesopotania, Sumer, and
Babylon are built on mythological deities, but also contain the
primary wisdom of the warrior way, philosophy, creation myth, law
and ethics.

To begin with, it is clear that there were commandments or written
codes of law by the kings of Mesopotania. From about 2100 BC
which is over 4100 years ago, The Code of Ur-Nammu is the oldest
known tablet containing a law code surviving today. It was written
in the Sumerian language Further, Hammurabi 1810 BC – 1750
BC), who became the first king of the Babylonian Empire, extending
Babylon's control over Mesopotamia by winning a series of wars
against neighboring kingdoms. From his reign, the code of
Hammurabi was created and contained 282 laws, written by scribes
on 12 tablets and dated 1780 BC.

Stele of <u>Naram-Sin</u>, (2240 BC) Sargon's grandson, celebrating his victory against the <u>Lullubi</u> from <u>Zagros</u> with his Horned Helmet and long beard.

Mesopotamian religious views were the first in recorded history. Mesopotamians believed that the universe or world was a flat disc, surrounded by a huge, holed space, and above that, heaven. Mesopotamians also believed that water was everywhere and that the universe was born from this enormous sea. In addition, Mesopotamian religion was both Henotheism and polytheistic. This means that there were many gods but Enlil was the most powerful.

Although the beliefs described above were held in common among Mesopotamians, there were also regional variations. For example, Sumer was the first civilization of record in Southern Iraq or Mesopotania. The Sumerian word for universe is an-ki, which refers to the god An and the goddess Ki. The primordial union of An and Ki produced Enlil, who became leader of the Sumerian pantheon. It is quite interesting that the Universe is a combination of masculine and feminine. Sumer is widely considered to be the earliest settled society in the world to have manifested all the features needed to qualify fully as a civilization, dating back approximately 7000 years ago. In Sumerian mythology, **Eridu** was said to be one of the five cities built before the flood. Eridu appears to be the earliest Sumerian settlement, founded ca. 4,900 BCE, close to the Persian Gulf near the mouth of the Euphrates River.

The son of the Gods An and Ki was named Enlil who was the air god. Mesopotamians believed that Enlil was the most powerful god. Enlil was the chief god of the Pantheon, much like the Greeks had Zeus and the Romans had Jupiter. The Sumerians also engaged various philosophical questions. The gods were said to have created humans from clay for the purpose of serving them. Moreover, in the time around 3000 BC, the civilizations and mysteries of Egypt would also become prominent.

The 20th century BC Akkadian writing called the **Atra-Hasis** which is named after its human hero, contains both a creation myth and a flood account. It is one of history's earliest writings. Tablet I contains a creation myth about the Sumerian gods Anu, Enlil and Enki, gods of sky, wind and water. Tablet II has issues about overpopulation of humans and the god Enlil sending famine and drought at intervals of every 1200 years to reduce the population. Tablet III of the Atrahasis Epic contains the flood story. This is the part that was adapted in the Epic of Gilgamesh which was written over 4000 years ago

Some Core Religious Practices and Beliefs of Mesopotamia

- Many gods and powerful deities, but one MOST powerful God.
- Laws and Ethics for the People (Commandments)
- Incantation and prayers offered to the God or Gods
- Astrology and use of the stars and heavens for speculation
- Festival Days and Cult worship of the primal Gods
- Sacrifices or gifts to praise the Gods

- Atonement to the Gods
- Building Shrines for Gods
- The Heart was the center of emotion and reason (Egyptian)
- That the spirit or soul was eternal.
- Talisman or Spiritual Symbols used to reinforce mental/spiritual connection
- Ancestor worship or reverence

God Ashur with Long Hair and Beard encircled by Winged Disc. Ashur and Marduk were worshipped some 3500 years ago after Hammurabi

Ancient Indo European-Iranian Religions

Zoroastrianism is the philisophical religion based on the teachings of the prophet Zoroaster. **Mazdaism** is the theology that observes the divine authority of Ahura Mazda, recognized by Zoroaster.

Basic Zoroastrian beliefs dating from roughly 1000 BC

1)   There is only one universal and transcendental God, Ahura Mazda, who is the one uncreated creator and to whom all praise and worship is directed.

2)   Ahura Mazda's creation — seen as *asha*, truth and order — is the opposite of chaos, evident as *druj*, falsehood and disorder. The resulting conflict involves the entire universe, including humanity, which has a role to play in this enduring conflict.

3)   Active engagement and participation in life through good thoughts, words and deeds is important to ensure happiness and to keep the chaos at bay. This *active* participation is a central element in Zoroaster's concept of free will, and Zoroastrianism generally rejected all forms of monasticism i.e. monk lifestyle

4)   Ahura Mazda will ultimately prevail, at which point the universe will undergo a cosmic renovation and time will end (*cf:* Zoroastrian eschatology). In the final renovation, all of creation will be reunited in Ahura Mazda.

5)   In Zoroasterism, the BAD is represented by Angra Mainyu, the "Destructive Principle", while the GOOD is represented through Ahura Mazda's Spenta Mainyu, the instrument or "Abundant Principle" of the act of creation. It is through GOOD that Ahura Mazda is permeates humankind & the Creator interacts with the world.

6)   As facets of Creation, Ahura Mazda emanated seven "sparks", the Amesha Spentas, "Bounteous Immortals" that are each the representative of one aspect of Creation. These Amesha Spenta are assisted by a league of lesser principles called the Yazatas, each "Worthy of Worship" and each again a foundation of a moral or physical aspect of creation.

Native American Spirituality

Because there were so many tribes and nations of American Indians in North and Latin America, we are going to use this section to list some contemplative quotes from famous American Indians or their leaders and Chiefs.

1) As John Mohawk most eloquently expressed:

The natural world is our bible. We don't have chapters and verses; we have trees and fish and animals. The creation is the manifestation of energy through matter. Because the universe is made up of manifestations of energy, the options for that manifestation are infinite. But we have to admit that the way it has manifested itself is organised. In fact, it is the most intricate organisation. We can't know how we impact on its law; we can talk only about how its law impacts upon us. We can make no judgement about nature.

The Indian sense of natural law is that nature informs us and it is our obligation to read nature as you would a book, to feel nature as you would a poem, to touch nature as you would yourself, to be a part of that and step into its cycles as much as you can.

2) Big Thunder (Bedagi) Wabanaki Algonquin

The Great Spirit is in all things, he is in the air we breathe. The Great Spirit is our Father, but the Earth is our Mother. She nourishes us, that which we put into the ground she returns to us....

3) Black Elk Oglala Sioux Holy Man - 1863-1950

You have noticed that everything as Indian does is in a circle, and that is because the Power of the World always works in circles, and everything tries to be round..... The Sky is round, and I have heard that the earth is round like a ball, and so are all the stars. The wind, in its greatest power, whirls. Birds make their nest in circles, for theirs is the same religion as ours....

Even the seasons form a great circle in their changing, and always come back again to where they were. The life of a man is a circle from childhood to childhood, and so it is in everything where power moves.

4) Lone Man (Isna-la-wica) Teton Sioux

... I have seen that in any great undertaking it is not enough for a man to depend simply upon himself.

5) In his book, *The Earth Shall Weep*, James Wilson expands his thoughts on Native American Creation Myth.:

Yet for all their range and variety, these stories often have a similar feel to them. When you set them alongside the biblical Genesis, the common features suddenly appear in sharp relief; they seem to glow with the newness and immediacy of creation, offering vivid explanations for the behaviour of an animal, the shape of a rock or a mountain, which you can still encounter in the here and now. Many tribes and nations call themselves, in their own languages, 'the first people', the 'original people', or the 'real people', and their stories place them firmly in a place of special power and significance...Far from telling them that they are locked out of Eden, the Indians' myths confirm that (unless they have been displaced by European contact and settlement) they still live in the place for which they were made; either the site of their own emergence or creation, or a 'Promised Land' which they have attained through long migration.

6) Chief Aupumut, Mohican. 1725

"When it comes time to die, be not like those whose hearts are filled with the fear of death, so when their time comes they weep and pray for a little more time to live their lives over again in a different way. Sing your death song, and die like a hero going home."

7) <u>Sitting Bull Hunkpapa Sioux</u>

"I am a red man. If the Great Spirit had desired me to be a white man he would have made me so in the first place. He put in your heart certain wishes and plans, in my heart he put other and different desires. Each man is good in his sight. It is not necessary for Eagles to be Crows. We are poor..but we are free. No white man controls our footsteps. If we must die...we die defending our rights."

As a special note, if you compare the Shinto, Norse and some Native American Cosmologies, you have amazing similarities such as:

1. Various Worlds in the Cosmology (Beyond Heaven and Hell)
2. World Tree's
3. Animal Spirits, Fetches or Fettishes
4. Shamanic Priests
5. Various Gods with Special Power
6. Sacred Types of Panenthiesm and Regard for Nature where the God or All Father/Mother flows permeates everything.
7. Heaven and a place for Gods and Warriors

Tibetan Buddhism

Tibetan Buddhism includes both Hinayana and Mahayana practices. However, Tibetan Buddhism practice is built around Vajrayana practices. Tibetan Buddhism is a complex philosophical and ritual framework to assist the seeking in their path towards enlightenment. Buddhism became a major presence in Tibet towards the end of the 8th century CE where it was brought from India at the invitation of the Tibetan king, Trisong Detsen, who invited two Buddhist masters to Tibet and had important Buddhist texts translated into Tibetan.

The Basic Teachings of Buddha which are core to Buddhism are: The Three Universal Truths; The Four Noble Truths; and • The Noble Eightfold Path

Tibetan Buddhism adheres to classic Buddhist principles such as Anātman (Sanskrit) or Anatta (not-self, bdag med), the five aggregates (phung po) karma and rebirth. Tibetan Buddhists also uphold various doctrines associated with Mahāyāna and the tantric Vajrayāna tradition.

The Bodhisattva path

A central representation for spiritual advancement used in Tibetan Buddhism is that of the five paths:

1. The path of preparation - Is attained when one reaches the union of calm abiding and higher insight meditations (see below) and one becomes familiar with emptiness.
2. The path of seeing - one perceives emptiness directly, all thoughts of subject and object are overcome, one becomes an arya.
3. The path of accumulation where the seeker collects wisdom and merit, generates bodhicitta, cultivates the four foundations of mindfulness and right effort ("four abandonments").

4. The path of meditation - one removes confusion from one's mind and perfects one's understanding.
5. The path of perfections or no more learning - which culminates in Buddhahood.

Special features -of Tibetan Buddhism

1. Tibetan Buddhism makes use of mandalas, mantras, mudras, and prayer wheels
2. The status of the teacher or "Lama"
3. Rich visual symbolism
4. Focus on the relationship between life and death
5. Important role of rituals and initiations
6. Elements of earlier Shamanic or Tibetan faiths
7. Mantras and meditation practice
8. The Dali Lama is leader of the Yellow Hats Sect.

(The Virtuous School) Founded by Tsong Khapa Lobsang Drakpa (also known as Je Rinpoche) (1357 - 1419). This school is headed by the Dalai Lama. Nyingmapa: Founded by Padmasambhava, this is oldest sect, noted in the West for the teachings of the Tibetan Book of the Dead.

Rituals

Rituals and simple spiritual practices such as mantras are popular with lay Tibetan Buddhists. They include prostrations, making offerings to statues of Buddhas or bodhisattvas, attending public teachings and ceremonies.

Tibetan temple ceremonies are often loud and visually impressive, with instruments, cymbals and gongs, and musical and chanting by formally dressed monks within temples and monasteries.

Vajrayāna

Tibetan Buddhism is a form of Buddhist Tantra, affirming the views in the texts known as the Buddhist Tantras (dating from around the 7th century CE onwards).

Tantra generally refers to forms of religious practice which focuses on the use of visualization, ideas, symbols and rituals for inner transformation. An important element of Tantric practice are tantric deities and their mandalas. Study of Buddhist Indian texts is key to the curriculum of all four major schools of Tibetan Buddhism. Memorization of classic texts is expected as part of traditional monastic education. The sacred writings were mostly finalized in the 13th century, and divided into two parts, the Kangyur (containing sutras and tantras) and the Tengyur (containing shastras and commentaries). The Nyingma school also maintains a separate collection of texts called the Nyingma Gyubum, assembled by Ratna Lingpa in the 15th century and revised by Jigme Lingpa.[88]

In Tibetan Buddhism, practices are generally classified as either Sutra (or Pāramitāyāna) or Tantra (Vajrayāna or Mantrayāna), though exactly what constitutes each category and what is included and excluded in each is a matter of debate and differs among the various lineages. According to Tsongkhapa for example, what separates Tantra from Sutra is the practice of Deity yoga.[99]

Tibetan Book of the Dead

This is one of the great texts of Tibetan Buddhism, and a big seller in the west. The English title is not a translation of the Tibetan title - the book's true name is Great Liberation through hearing during the intermediate state, commonly known in Tibet as Liberation through hearing. The book deals with the experiences of a person as they pass between death and rebirth.

Zen Buddhism

Zen Buddhism is a mixture of Mahayana Buddhism from India and Taoism. It began in China, spread to Japan and Korea, and became popular in the West from the mid 20th century. The foundation of Zen is attempting to understand the meaning of life directly, without being misled by logic or materialistic thought or language.

Zen emphasizes rigorous meditation-practice, insight into Buddha-nature, and the living the principles in daily life, especially for the benefit of others. As such, it de-emphasizes mere knowledge of sutras and doctrine and favors direct understanding through Zazen and interaction with an accomplished teacher.

Zen incorporates the Buddhist pantheon, and teaches that the divine nature is in all things and that Buddha-nature is shared by everyone

Some Zen Practices

Observing the breath

During sitting meditation you may assume a position such as lotus position, half-lotus, Burmese, or seiza postures. For the regulation of the mind, awareness is directed towards counting numbers or watching yourbreath or by bringing your awareness to your energy center below the navel chakra. Sometimes, a cushion placed on a padded mat is used to sit on or a chair may be used.

Observing the mind

In some schools of Zen, meditation with no objects, anchors, or content, is a fundamental form of practice. The seeker strives to be aware of their stream of thoughts, allowing their thoughts to arise and pass without interference. Considerable textual, philosophical, and phenomenological ideas about this practice can be found in the "Principles of Zazen" or the "Universally Recommended Instructions for Zazen". In Japanese languages, this practice is called Shikantaza.

At the beginning of the Song Dynasty, practice with the kōan method became popular.

A kōan, literally "public case", is a fable or dialogue, describing an interaction between a master and student. These anecdotes give a demonstration of the master's insight. Koans emphasize the non-conceptional ideas that Buddhist teachings are illuminating. Koans can be used to provoke thought, facination, "great doubt", and test a student's Zen practice.

Interesting things about ZEN

1. The first real Zen Master was probably Hui-Neng 637-713AD

2. 8% of Japanese Buddhists identify with ZEN

3. Zen Buddhism has influenced Poetry, Prose, Tea Ceremonies, Ceramics, Architecture, and more

4. Soto Zen emphasizes zazen (sitting meditation) but Rinzai Zen also uses koans or riddles to help practitioners achieve enlightenment.

5. The most famous Koan is, "What is the sound of one hand clapping"

6. Japanese received Buddhism in the sixth century and Japanese Buddhism now contains a mixture of: Confucianism, Shinto, and Chinese Busshism.

Shinto:

Shinto (神道 Shintō) is the name for the non-Buddhist religious practices of the region of Japan. The word Shinto means ("Way of the Gods") combining "shin" (神), meaning gods or spirits ; and "tō" (道), meaning "do", or a philosophical study (originally from the Chinese word tao).

The people of ancient Japan had various animistic beliefs, worshipped divine ancestors and communicated with spirit worlds via shamans like many other EurAsian cultures (c. 300 BCE - 300 CE).

In Shinto, the gods, spirits, supernatural forces or essences are known as Kami which govern nature in all forms where they are believed to inhabit all beauty on Earth.

Sources on early Shinto beliefs include the Manyoshu or 'Collection of 10,000 Leaves.' Written around 760 CE, this is a compilation of poems covering all manner of topics similar to psalms or eddas.

Purity

Shinto teaches specific deeds may create ritual impurity that we should want catharsis to maintain peace of mind and good fortune.

Baptismal Rites

Whena baby is born in Japan, a local Shinto shrine will come to add the child's name to the shrine and then declare him or her part of the family or a "family child" (氏子 ujiko).

Clans

Historically, the constituent body of Shinto society was the uji (clan). The head of each Uji was in charge of the worship of the clan's ujigami or also known as the particular localized guardian deity much like the ancient Sumerian city-gods. Like many cultures, there are high festivals which include a prayer for good harvest in spring and the harvest ceremony in autumn honouring the ujigami.

Fusion with Buddhism

Around the 8th century, Shintō began to import ideas from a Buddhist viewpoint. Shintō kami became protectors of Buddhism; hence, shrines for kami were built within the precincts of Buddhist temples. Shintō, literally means "the way of kami" and the gods within Shinto are called kami.

Gods

Shintoism recognizes thousands of Gods called KAMI. There are three key gods and goddesses. Izanagi and Izanami are the original two kami. Male/female counterparts, Izanagi and Izanami represent duality of nature and their union created the cosmos and the islands of Japan. There are other original kami who represented elemental forces like fire.

Principles

Shinto religion emphasizes four principle values:

1. Maintenance of family traditions

2. Love of nature

3. Physical orderliness & cleanliness

4. Worship of the Kami

Heaven and Bridge to Heaven

In Shinto, Takamagahara (or Takama no Hara) is the dwelling place of the heavenly gods (amatsukami). It is believed to be connected to the Earth by the bridge Ama-no-uki-hashi (the "Floating Bridge of Heaven"). Similarly, in Eurasian Norse mythology, which is a whopping 8,437 km distance from Tokoyo, the Scandanavians also have a heaven for the Gods and a special bridge called Bifrost along with a reverence for divine ancestors.

Confucianism

Confucianism also known as Ruism is an ethical and philosophical system, also described as a religion. Confucianism revolves around the pursuit of the unity of the self & the God of Heaven (Tiān 天), or around the relationship between humanity and Heaven. The principle of Heaven (Lǐ 理 or Dào 道), is the source of divine authority, monistic in its structure.

Confucius, romanization Kongfuzi or K'ung-fu-tzu (born 551, Qufu, state of Lu or Shandong province, China —died 479 BCE, Lu), As China's most famous teacher, philosopher, and political theorist, his philosophy and ethics have influenced the civilization of East Asia.

There are vast works in Confucian literature including: Five Classics, The Book of History, The Book of Poetry and Songs, The Book of Changes and The Book of Rites.

Confucian ethics are humanistic. This ethical philosophy can be applied to all the members of a society. Confucian ethics are duties and virtues encompassed by the Five Constants, or the Wuchang (五常), as written by Confucian scholars during the Han Dynasty. The Five Constants are:

1. Rén (仁, humaneness);

2. Yì (義, righteousness or justice);

3. Lǐ (禮, proper rite);

4. Zhì (智, knowledge);

5. Xìn (信, integrity).

These are accompanied by the classical Sìzì (四字), that singles out four virtues, one of which is included among the Five Constants:

1. Zhōng (忠, loyalty);

2. Xiào (孝, filial piety);

3. Jié (節, continency);

4. Yì (義, righteousness).

Confucius believed that social disorder often stemmed from failure to perceive, understand, and deal with reality. Fundamentally, then, social disorder can stem from the failure to call things by their proper names, and his solution to this was zhèngmíng. A key Confucian concept is that in order to govern others one must first govern oneself according to the universal order.

Some interesting things abotu Confucianism:

1. Harmony depends on the five great relationships

2. People have the potential for good and needed cultivation

3. Government would improve if more philosphers worked in government

4. The great importance of JEN or human heartedness and li which is correct ceremony.

5. At the root of Confucianism is SHU which is the principle of reciprocity.

Other Principles of High Values of Confucianism Are:

1. World Peace

2. National Order

3. Regulation of the Family

4. Cultivation of the individual

5. Perfection of the Mind or Mental Orderliness

6. Sincerey of the will

7. Knowledge and Wisdom

8. Investigation into the reality and causes of things.

Comparison Chart for Eastern EurAsian Religions					
Name of Religion	Country of Origin	Date of Origin	Name of Founder	Title of Founder	Social Position and/or Avocation
Hinduism	India	Prehistoric	***	***	***
Shintoism	Japan	Prehistoric	***	***	***
Zoroastrianism	Persia (Iran)	7th cent. B.C.	Zarathustra Zoroaster		
Taoism	China	6th cent. B.C.	Li-poh-Yang	Lao-Tze	Court Librarian and Recoder; Historian
Confucianism	China	6th cent. B.C.	Kung Fu-Tzu	The Perfect	Teacher, Minor Posts,
			(Confucius)	Sage	Soldier, Father
Jainism	India	Prehistoric	Varhamana	Mahavira	Kshatriya Caste
Buddhism	India	6th cent. B.C.	Siddartha	Buddha Enlightened One	Kshatriya Caste
Sikhism	India	15th cent. A.D.	Nanak	Baba (Father)	Kshatriya Caste

Gnosticism

In 1945, there were 53 Gnostic Texts discovered in a cave in Egypt and are called the **Nag Hammadi library** (popularly known as **The Gnostic Gospels**). These documents shed great light upon the Christian Church in its infancy. The main focus of the Gnostics was that the Christian experience was a question of knowing or knowledge. Thus, a personal experience with the divine, and not only an experience with dogma or priests. The Gnostics believe that the world could only be improved by each person transforming themselves. Therefore, the Gnostics advocated an action based faith with works and not just a creed based on hope or wishful aspirations. Gnostics may have also believed that all simple apparent realities are an illusion which could be a "false god". The Gnostics also referred to the feminine aspects of God in their references to Sophia or wisdom. This issue is still addressed in Christian texts today such as the Apocrypha, but not much is taught on the subject in most catechisms. [vi]

Some Gnostic Beliefs

- The notion of a remote, supreme monadic divinity. In many Gnostic systems, God is known as the Monad, the One, The Absolute.
- A benevolent creator of the universe.
- Jesus of Nazareth is identified by some Gnostic sects as an embodiment of the supreme being who became incarnate to bring gnosis to the Earth
- A person attains salvation by learning secret knowledge
- Gnostics tended to believe that Christ and his teachings were to liberate the people along with allowing persons to free their soul or spirit to return to the creator at death.
- Humans are divine souls trapped in a material world created by an imperfect spirit.
- The Kingdom of God is within the Individual and must be tapped into.

14 Spiritual Principles of the Warrior

1.   ***Illusion Energy and Reality*** -- We are living in the illusion where we are separated from our divine inheritance of being spiritually awake. Our goal is to regenerate our souls through this PROCESS, and realize that the spirit/self that lies within us is the divine connection that propels us to our natural and highest livelihood. This separation limits our abilities as we are limited by our ego-mind. Evaluating our history and track record with honesty, we can see that we have much more potential. We then should learn how to grow and leave behind unproductive living and attitudes. How can we head toward wholeness, peace and prosperity? Through transformation and optimization of our minds, one can meet their true inner Self which is connected to the Spirit of the Universe. We are all part of the Force or Spiritual Energy of The Universe. Without our spirit, our mind and bodies would not be animated, filled with ideas, and alive. We become awake spiritually and realize that All is right with our world, and we apply the highest and most constructive truth to our world view.

• " There are as many pillows of illusion as flakes in a snowstorm. We wake from one dream into another dream. " Ralph Waldo Emerson

• A wise man, recognizing that the world is but an illusion, does not act as if it is real, so he escapes the suffering. – The Buddha

• "Neither shall they say, Lo here! or, lo there! for, behold, the kingdom of God is within you." (Luke 17:21)

• "The real self (**atman**) is distinct from the temporary body. One must go beyond the illusion of ego and self, to find their true essence and soul." ~ Magus Incognito

• The Bhagavad-Gita states our atman... the supreme consciousness that invades whole cosmic system is the only truth of life! Our atman soul is the truthful master and controller of body.

• "Sometimes, simply by sitting, the soul collects wisdom." ~Zen proverb

• Fantasies are the veil behind which truth is hidden. (ACIM p. 316)
• "Don't be satisfied with stories, how things have gone with others. Unfold your own myth." — Rumi, Essential Rumi

2. ***Perception – Gratitude Enthusiasm and Optimism*** - Our aliveness and well being is based on our spiritual condition which is based on the operative, optimal- mechanics of our mind (ability to see and perceive). At present, we are limited to the primitive view of only that which is surface reality and apparent, and we must evolve to be able to see beyond what is obvious. Liberation takes effort; thus, "A better view generates a better journey". We must transcend our separation and our ego to become in tune with our authentic selves and see past the illusion.

Quotes:
• Finally, brethren, whatsoever things are true, whatsoever things are honest, whatsoever things are just, whatsoever things are pure, whatsoever things are lovely, whatsoever things are of good report; if there be any virtue, and if there be any praise, think on these things. Philippians 4:8
• "The first gulp from the glass of natural sciences will turn you into an atheist, but at the bottom of the glass God is waiting for you." — Werner Heisenberg – World Renowned Physicist
• The mind can be the source of bondage, or can be the source of liberation. (Maitri Upanishad)
• Come to me, all who labor and are heavy laden, and I will give you rest. Take my yoke upon you, and learn from me, for I am gentle and lowly in heart, and you will find rest for your souls. For my yoke is easy, and my burden is light." Matthew 11:28-30

Clarity and Perception Quotes

JESUS	KRISHNA
Unless one is born anew, he will not be able to see the kingdom of God... unless one is born of water and the Spirit, he cannot enter the Kingdom of God. That which is born of flesh is flesh. That which is born of spirit, spirit is. **The Gospel of John**	All things born in truth must die, but out of death comes life. **The Bagavad Gita**

BUDDHA	LAO TZU
The cessation of the discriminating mind cannot take place until there is a "turning-about in the deepest seat of consciousness. **The Lankavatara Sutra**	In gathering your vital energy so that you can create agility, have you achieved the state of a new-born child? In cleansing your inner vision, have you purified all of its dullness? **The Tao Te Ching**

3.   *Unity and The Way Home* - To connect to the power of
the universe, we must be fined tuned into our individual spirit which

connects us to the Universal Spirit. **FLOW** - Through a catharsis,
purification, forgiveness, we obtain wholeness and clarity.

Quotes

• When practicing contemplation, They should wish that all beings, See
truth as it is
And be forever free of oppression and contention. -Buddhism. *Garland
Sutra, 11*

• Lord of Creation! No one other than Thee pervades all these that have
come into being. May that be ours for which our prayers rise, may we
be masters of many treasures!
-Hinduism. *Rig Veda, 10.121.10*

• If the poorest of mankind come here once for worship, I will surely
grant their hearts' desire.
-Shinto. *Oracle of Itsukushima*

• "But seek ye first the kingdom of God and His righteousness," he
declared, "and all these things shall be added unto you" (Matthew
6:33).

• *"Be the change that you wish to see in the world." — Mahatma Gandhi*

4.   ***The Present***- Cultivating positive energy, we tune in and
obtain connectedness which affords us divine flow, ideas, and clarity.
Our inner voice is clear when our mind is clear. This transparency
allows for better decisions in seizing upon your ideas.

Quotes

- Jesus said to him, "No one who puts his hand to the plow and looks
  back is fit for the kingdom of God." Luke 9:62
- "If you are depressed, you are living in the past. If you are anxious, you
  are living in the future. If you are at peace, you are living in the
  present."   ~ Lao Tzu
- "Not what we have But what we enjoy, constitutes our abundance."
  ~Epicurus quotes (Greek philosopher, BC 341-270)
- Do not dwell in the past, do not dream of the future, concentrate the
  mind on the present moment. ~ Buddha

- Our wealth is rewarded in direct proportion to the number of people with whom we are willing to share. ~ Paul Zane Pilzer
- "Yesterday is gone. Tomorrow has not yet come. We have only today. Let us begin." — Mother Teresa

5. ***Spiritual Freedom and Beyond the Ego*** – Taming of the Mind, Spirit before Ego. A holy-spirit connection provides awareness when we are able to put our spiritual path before our ego mind. This awareness is the sixth sense of seeing and thought management.

Quotes
- The ego cannot survive without judgment. (ACIM p. 54)
- "The foundation of the Buddha's teachings lies in compassion, and the reason for practicing the teachings is to wipe out the persistence of ego, the number-one enemy of compassion."~ Tenzin Gyatso, the 14th Dalai Lama
- In the secret cave of the heart, two are seated by life's fountain. The separate ego drinks of the sweet and bitter stuff, Liking the sweet, disliking the bitter, While the supreme Self drinks sweet and bitter. Neither liking this nor disliking that. The ego gropes in darkness, while the Self lives in light. ~ Quote / Poem n° 3217 : Upanishads, Hinduism
- "Don't compare yourself with anyone in this world...if you do so, you are insulting yourself." — Bill Gates
- So Jesus said to them, "Truly, truly, I say to you, the Son can do nothing of his own accord, but only what he sees the Father doing. For whatever the Father does, that the Son does likewise. John 5:19
- Part of being a winner is knowing when enough is enough. Sometimes you have to give up the fight and walk away, and move on to something that's more productive. ~ Donald Trump

6.   ***Potential in the Now*** - To maximize awake-ness, we must compartmentalize our day. Each day gives us new lessons and life's challenges. We learn and we grow. With contemplative action, we can enter the 4th dimension of living.   We defragment our minds and souls through a practical, psychological clearing process. Using this process, we eliminate and mitigate non-productive thoughts. We must banish blame, put aside blocks to our happiness, learn to stop distractions, and begin to engage true focus on our growth and happiness. We begin to release instinctual judgments of people, places and things. This is where liberation begins.

Quotes on Potential

- The will to win, the desire to succeed, the urge to reach your full potential... these are the keys that will unlock the door to personal excellence. ~ Confucius
- Jesus: "Those who want to save their life will lose it, and those who lose their life for my sake will save it." Mark 8:35
- Buddha: "With the relinquishing of all thought and egotism, the enlightened one is liberated through not clinging." Majjhima Nikaya 72:15
- "Always dream and shoot higher than you know you can do. Do not bother just to be better than your contemporaries or predecessors. Try to be better than yourself." ~ William Faulkner
- "The starting point of all achievement is DESIRE. Keep this constantly in mind. Weak desire brings weak results, just as a small fire makes a small amount of heat." — Napoleon Hill, Think and Grow Rich

7.   ***PURPOSE*** – FOCUS, CONCENTRATION, MEANING - Transcend fear, scarcity, anger, frustration and lack. Abundance and faith is an inside job and esoteric procedure. By eliminating these blocks to the sunlight of the spirit, we approach unity with our spiritual self which is connected to the force of the universe.

Quotes

- "He who has a why to live for can bear almost any how." ~ Friedrich Nietzsche
- "Your purpose in life is to find your purpose and give your whole heart and soul to it" ~ Gautama Buddha
- Our prime purpose in this life is to help others. And if you can't help them, at least don't hurt them. ~ Dalai Lama
- "The purpose of art is washing the dust of daily life off our souls". ~ Pablo Picasso
- Any idea, plan, or purpose may be placed in the mind through repetition of thought. ~ Napoleon Hill
- There is one quality which one must possess to win, and that is definiteness of purpose, the knowledge of what one wants, and a burning desire to possess it. ~ Napoleon Hill
- "We are products of our past, but we don't have to be prisoners of it." ~ Rick Warren, The Purpose Driven Life: What on Earth Am I Here for?
- Success is not final, failure is not fatal: it is the courage to continue that counts. ~ Winston Churchill

8. *Harmony – Peace of Mind and Forgiveness* —

We must cleanse our mind and senses by working through our past and developing harmonious thinking. We then can grow closer to peace of mind and our natural purpose. The goal is to unfold and become what we are meant to be. We are to fully express our life and potentiality.

Quotes

• Jesus said, **"And when you stand praying, if you hold anything against anyone, forgive him, so that your Father in heaven may forgive you your sins" (Mark 11:25).**

• "Peace comes from within. Do not seek it without." — Gautama Buddha

• "Nothing external to you has any power over you." — Ralph Waldo Emerson

• "Pleasure is always derived from something outside you, whereas joy arises from within." — Eckhart Tolle

• "The wise man does not lay up his own treasures. The more he gives to others, the more he has for his own." Lao Tzu

• He abused me, he struck me, he overcame me, he robbed me' -- in those who do not harbor such thoughts hatred will cease. (Dhammapada 1.3-4; translation. w:Radhakrishnan).

• "Be kind and compassionate to one another, forgiving each other, just as in Christ God forgave you." (Ephesians 4:32)

• "When you hold resentment toward another, you are bound to that person or condition by an emotional link that is stronger than steel. Forgiveness is the only way to dissolve that link and get free." — Catherine Ponder

• If one who has been wronged by another does not wish to rebuke or speak to the offender – because the offender is simple or confused – then if he sincerely forgives him, neither bearing him ill-will nor administering a reprimand, he acts according to the standard of the pious. (Deot 6:9).

• "A big part of financial freedom is having your heart and mind free from worry about the what-ifs of life." — Suze Orman

9.   ***Creativity*** - Relationships must become harmonious and driven by harmlessness while being inspired by our spiritual giving selves. Generally, we are driven to be over-dependent, defiant, or rebellious toward others. Beging anew, we can now operate from a spiritual, prosperous, clear and authentic place, we can transcend these instincts and respond in a spiritual way rather than react to others in relations.

Quotes

- Whatever you can do, or dream you can do, begin it. Boldness has genius, power, and magic in it. Begin it now to heat the mind and complete the tasks... ~ **Goethe**
- "It is better to live your own destiny imperfectly than to live an imitation of somebody else's life with perfection." ~ Anonymous, The Bhagavad Gita
- Whatever you do, work heartily, as for the Lord and not for men. Colossians 3:23
- Burning desire to be or do something gives us staying power - a reason to get up every morning or to pick ourselves up and start in again after a disappointment. ~ Marsha Sinetar Do what you love and the money will follow.
- "The painter has the Universe in his mind and hands." — Leonardo da Vinci
- "As my sufferings mounted I soon realized that there were two ways in which I could respond to my situation -- either to react with bitterness or seek to transform the suffering into a creative force. I decided to follow the latter course." — Martin Luther King Jr.

Visualization – With the development of our imagination, we learn to picture our goals and dreams in our mind. We further discover how to cultivate a feeling that "All is right with my World" Begin at home and learn to build relationships with complements, praise and support. Prayer and visualization and feeling are linked on a spiritual and universal level. An affirmation or prayer should be utilized in a way that invokes feeling and energy to the core of your spirit. This can be called cognitive cellular transformation CCT.   Using prayer, visualization and affirmations must be optimized so that your consciousness is lifted up. If you must hit your knees or gently tap your chest while praying, these techniques can help infuse your spirit with a higher energy and higher connection with the spiritual source of all. Seeing the results of your visualization or affirmation in your mind's eye is part of the visualization process. Feeling what you see in your mind's eye is yet another step.

Visualization Quotes:

* Now faith is the assurance of things hoped for, the conviction of things not seen. For by it the people of old received their commendation. By faith we understand that the universe was created by the word of God, so that what is seen was not made out of things that are visible. Hebrews 11:1-3
* Jesus answered him, "Truly, truly, I say to you, unless one is born again he cannot see the kingdom of God." John 3:3
* "I learned this, at least, by my experiment: that if one advances confidently in the direction of his dreams, and endeavors to live the life which he has imagined, he will meet with a success unexpected in common hours." — Henry David Thoreau, Walden: Or, Life in the Woods

10.   ***Contemplation Prayer & Meditation*** - Seek inspiration and quiet time. Find the flow and connection to the Spirit of the Universe. Seek your authentic voice of ideas. Learn how to take affirmative action toward your dreams. Learn to speak your truth. Learn to pray for protection, and contemplate love, health and wealth. Develop a higher consciousness and connectedness. Contemplation is also key because it affords us time to develop receptivity. Receptivity means that we develop an openness to the flow of ideas to us and allow ourselves to be perceptive enough to see signs in which to act upon.

Contemplation Quotes:
* "When meditation is mastered, the mind is unwavering, like the flame of a lamp in a windless place." ~ **Krishna**
* "Meditation in its essence is the art of seeing into the nature of one's being, and it points the way from bondage to freedom." ~ **DT Suzuki**
* Right understanding, with true longing, absolute trust, and sweet grace-giving mindfulness ~ ***Julian of Norwich***
* The function of prayer is not to influence God, but rather to change the nature of the one who prays." — Søren Kierkegaard

• "If the only prayer you said was thank you, that would be enough." — Meister Eckhart
• The memory of God comes to the quiet mind. (ACIM p. 457)

11. ***Character Inventory*** - We must limit our blocks to freedom as well as our character flaws. Continuously evaluate what works and what does not work. We must begin using what works each day based on the success of actions, inactions and thinking. Practice these steps so that you can optimize your knowingness of the Spirit of the Universe. Get and Stay lucid, release peace, radiate love.

Inventory and Self Analysis Quotes:

• "He who knows others is wise; he who knows himself is enlightened." — Lao Tzu
• Therefore, confess your sins to one another and pray for one another, that you may be healed. The prayer of a righteous person has great power as it is working. James 5:16
• "No one is free who has not obtained the empire of himself. No man is free who cannot command himself." — Pythagoras
• 1 John 1:9 If we confess our sins, he is faithful and just to forgive us our sins and to cleanse us from all unrighteousness.
• James 5:16 Therefore, confess your sins to one another and pray for one another, that you may be healed. The prayer of a righteous person has great power as it is working.
• Proverbs 28:13 Whoever conceals his transgressions will not prosper, but he who confesses and forsakes them will obtain mercy.
• The weak can never forgive. Forgiveness is the attribute of the strong. Mahatma Gandhi
• Do not be conformed to this world, but be transformed by the renewal of your mind, that by testing you may discern what is the will of God, what is good and acceptable and perfect. ~ Romans 12:2

12. ***Character Development and Humility*** – Your
Mind and Body is your temple – We must learn to feed our body and
mind with only the things that will provide abundant and prosperous
emotions and ideas. Learn from lessons and continue to maximize your
potential. Our thinking is part of our character. We become what we
think. Constructive thinking based in gratitude can allow us to see the
best in life.

Character Development Quotes:

• Nearly all men can stand adversity, but if you want to test a man's
character, give him power. **Abraham Lincoln**

• Character cannot be developed in ease and quiet. Only through
experience of trial and suffering can the soul be strengthened, ambition
inspired, and success achieved. **Helen Keller**

• Character is higher than intellect. A great soul will be strong to live as
well as think. **Ralph Waldo Emerson**

• Our characters are the result of our conduct. Aristotle, Nicomachean
Ethics (c. 335 B.C).

• Our character is the totality of our thinking, actions and inactions.
Our goal is to develop the power to maximize our character. ~ **Magus
Incognito – Essays**

• Only by strict specialization can the scientific worker become fully
conscious, for once and perhaps never again in his lifetime, that he has
achieved something that will endure. A really definitive and good
accomplishment is today always a specialized act. ~ Max Weber

• *Es bildet ein Talent sich in der Stille, Sich ein Charakter in dem Strom
der Welt.* "Talent is nurtured in solitude; character is formed in the
stormy billows of the world." ~ Johann Wolfgang von Goethe, *Torquato
Tasso*, I, 2, 66.

13.   ***LOVE*** - When we are in flow, tuned in to our spiritual selves, we realize that GOD is LOVE.   Love is patient, kind, unselfish, giving, generous, humble, understanding, thankful, grateful, compassionate, and more. Using these virtues is pure Wisdom. Become "in love" with your soul and the Spirit of the Universe. Miracles occur naturally as expressions of love. They are performed by those who temporarily have more for those who temporarily have less. (ACIM p. 1) Love dissipates resentments and affords forgiveness and clarity. T 1 A 2. The course does not aim at teaching the meaning of love, for that is beyond what can be taught. It does aim, however, at removing the blocks to the awareness of Love's Presence, Which is your natural inheritance. The opposite of love is fear, but what is all-encompassing can have no opposite.

Quotes on Love
- "Your task is not to seek for love, but merely to seek and find all the barriers within yourself that you have built against it." — Rumi
- You may receive love from many, but until you learn to give it & truly radiate love to others, you will not see the spark of life and joy that surrounds you. ~ Magus Incognito
- Greater love hath no man than this, that a man lay down his life for his friends. Jesus Christ, in John 15:13
- "Since the only Presence and Power of the Universe loves me and sustains me, what on earth could I possibly fear? Nothing. No - thing. Love heals, love prospers, love protects, love gaurds, love guides, love restores, love creates, love makes all things new. So I let love go before me now to straighten out every crooked place in my life. I place my faith in God's love for me, and I am free, as I was created to be." -John Randolph Price from "The Love Book"
- TO LOVE is to find pleasure in the happiness of others. Gottfried Leibniz, A Dialogue (c. 1696).
- Perfect love casts out fear. If fear exists, then there is not perfect love. (p.12)

<u>*Love Comparison Chart*</u>

JESUS CHRIST	KRISHNA
Love our neighbors a ourselves. **The Gospels of Mark, Matthew and John**	The true Yogi applies the same standard to others a he applies to himself. Seeing what is pleasure an pain for himself, he knows what is pleasure and pain for others. Thus, he wishe good to all and evil to none **The Bagavad Gita**
BUDDHA	LAO TZU
Being immersed in the highest state of consciousness, the disciple's heart is connected to compassion. He sees himself in all beings and is free from negative feelings toward others. **Doctrinal Formulas**	If we sacrifice this body fo the world's benefit, the all things will come to that person who loves others a he loves himself. **The Tao Te Ching**

14. ***Knowing*** - Be open to the power, healing and perfection of divine power and flow. When you have the knowingness and beingness, you are, in fact, filled with the holy spirit of the universe. You will then live in a higher order of being in the 4th dimension.

Knowingness Quotes:
• All who call on God in true faith, earnestly from the heart, will certainly be heard, and will receive what they have asked and desired. **Martin Luther**
• As for God, "I don't need to believe, <u>I Know</u>" – **Dr. Carl Jung**
• Develop an attitude of gratitude, and give thanks for everything that happens to you, knowing that every step forward is a step toward achieving something bigger and better than your current situation. ~ Brian Tracy
• The unwise man is awake all night worries over and again. When morning rises he is restless still, his burden as before. ~ The Havamal
• "Your beliefs become your thoughts, Your thoughts become your words, Your words become your actions, Your actions become your habits, Your habits become your values, Your values become your destiny." — Mahatma Gandhi
• "All I have seen teaches me to trust the Creator for all I have not seen." — Ralph Waldo Emerson

According to the Gospels, a Roman centurion asked Jesus for help because his boy servant was ill. Jesus offered to go to the centurion's house to perform the healing, but the centurion said, ""Lord, I do not deserve to have you come under my roof. But just say the word, and my servant will be healed." When Jesus heard this, he said to the people about the Roman Warrior: "Truly I tell you, I have not found anyone in Israel with such great faith."

Metaphysical Exercises

1)A Final Visualization Exercise for Results

1. In a quiet spot, enter your relaxed state of mind and take a few deep breaths.

2. Relax each part of the body, one by one.

3. Close your eyes and imagine a snapshot of something that you really want to happen in your life.

4. Detail the final result of this desire with your five senses. View and See it, Smell it, Hear it, Taste it, and Touch it in your MIND.

5. Imagine the emotions that you will have when this dream or goal or result is reached. Feel the emotions of joy and thankfulness.

6. Harvest the mental essence of how having the result or thing will function in your life, serve you, and help all involved.

7. Believe that it has happened in your mind and allow yourself to imagine the present ownership of this result mentally.

8. Pinpoint and focus on the completed final event of success. For example, "The foot race is completed," or "The check is in your bank account." You are also encouraged to imagine the incremental successes and steps being achieved along with the arrival at the final result.

9. Experience love and grateful feelings when you recognize and realize your vision. Know and feel it as if it is fact.

10. Imagine the benefits for all involved.

11. Be willing to receive all of this good on a mental and spiritual level, which allows you to take actions toward creating and receiving the results.

12. Make sure you have created ways to capture the result. Example: You may not be able to become the highest paid pilot without a license. Also, allow yourself to feel deserving and worthy of the result.

13. Send this mental vision into the world with joy as a mental letter delivered to the Supreme Architect.

14. Respond to communication from others and ponder your intuition. Be willing to meet others halfway and to go the extra mile.

15. Allow your dreams to unfold on parallel lines. Example: You may want a successful business in offering one product or service, but the laws of attraction and excellence may allow you to sell many other things related to it.

2) Character Building Exercises to Ask Yourself

1.   Are your spirit, mind, and body in an ideal condition? If not, what do you want to do this year to expand your present situation?

2.   Have you studied the things you wanted to learn about? Will you continue?

3.   Have you seen the things you are most interested in? The art, the places, the people?

4.   What type of career or careers are you most suited for? If you could pick two or three careers that you would love to do, what would they be?

5.   If you could not fail, what would you do with your life?

6.   Do you have anxiety or fears over your career or relationships? If so, why? What can you do to lower the stress and improve your enjoyment of life?

7.   How do you want to be treated by others? What can you do to improve the way you are perceived?

8.   Can you think of three people you have loved as a good friend?

9.   George Harrison said, "In the end, the love you make is equal to the love you take." Are you giving or radiating love? Are you giving a reasonable amount of love and praise to those you love?

10.   What is the one thing that you could improve about yourself that would make the greatest difference in your opportunity or appearance?

11.   At the end of your life, how would you want people to remember you?

12.   Where do you want to travel? What do you want to see before you get too old? What do you want your children to see?

13.   Remember five things that you are grateful for in your childhood—people, family, experiences, talents? Remember that feeling of awe, excitement, appreciation that you once had.

14.   If you could model yourself after one or two successful people, who would they be? And why?

15.   Who are you, how would you define yourself?

16.   Do you feel worthy of an excellent life? What could you do to improve your outlook on life?

17.   What five things can you do each day that would allow you to treat other people better and to feel better about yourself?

18.   What can you feed yourself to make you healthier, happier, and smarter? Food, news, literature, exercise, types of relationships?

19.   Name 10 hobbies or activities that you enjoy. Examples: puzzles, tennis, bowling, reciting poetry. Do some of them. Get out of your comfort zone.

20.   What spiritually inspires you? What makes you feel more in tune with the universe? What gives you peace and harmony? How could you donate your talent, time, or money to something that inspires you?

Spiritual Exercises

Concentration Exercise

1. Find a relaxed part of your home
2. Sit and quiet the mind and begin to relax each part of the body (that you can think of) from head to toes.
3. Shut your eyes & take a few deep breaths.
4. Think of a room that you lived in as a child or that you are presently in.
5. Begin to see and visualized in your mind the entire room and its contents and where things are located. (Whatever you can recall)
6. It is also good to imagine the exact color of things in the room with your eyes closed.
7. This is also a good exercise to do even after you have entered a new building or place.
8. Do this for a few minutes each day and your focus and concentration will increase. These days, there is computer software that actually runs programs to help concentration in this same way..
9. As a note, this same type of exercise is also very good to relax and vividly recall wonderful people or possessions that you have in your past or present.
- Open your eyes when done with any of these exercises ☺

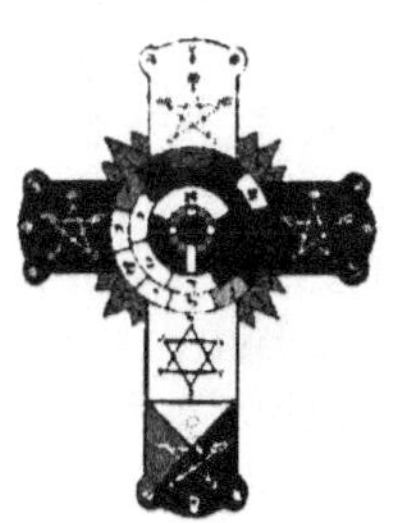

Active Meditation Exercise for Intuition and Guidance

1. Engage steps 1, 2 & 3 above.

2. With eyes closed and imagining, see yourself going into a sacred castle.
3. As you enter the main chamber, you see the (helpful person of your choice).
4. This person could be alive or from the past.
5. You then discuss with her or him in your minds eye. [imagination]
6. You ask questions and your Friendly Guru answers these questions.
7. Try and sense the answers from your core (heart and stomach).
8. When you are finished, thank your friend for the help and guidance.
9. You may have an overwhelming sense that this voice or person is from a higher or different viewpoint than your own.

Exercise for Energizing or Healing Yourself.

1) Engage steps 1,2, and 3 above. (Relaxing in a chair with spine straight) relax your hands on your lap.
2) Close your eyes and visualize a peaceful lake that has no ripples. Then see yourself surrounded by bright white particles of energy that also permeates your body.
3) In your mind, see the bright light move toward and focus on the area of discomfort or pain. Allow this white light to fill any affected area and flow thought your body.
4) Know that the white light brings all of your body's healing power to work most effectively for you.
5) Take a few breaths.
6) Then, allow this bright light to act like water and flow though your body.
7) Allow the "fluid of light" purify and wash the entire body.
8) Feel and see in your minds eye that the washing fluid of white light is "pure love" and cleanses you of ANY AND ALL fear, resentment, hurt, and dis-ease.
9) Say to yourself, I forgive myself and everyone for the past.

Thank the light of the universe for removing any impurities from your body.

10) Claim mental freedom from all problems in your mind and spirit. Thank the universe for your health and peace.
11) See others in your mind's eye walking up to you and congratulating you on your healing and success.
12) That's it..... & Open your eyes.
13) ** To do this exercise for others, pretend that they are the person in a chair in front of you as you have your eyes closed and send a mental request of peace and health for them.

Five Exercises to Augment Peace of Mind and Mental Abilities

One: get in a quiet place where there are no distractions and think of the alphabet. Think of a letter. Select the letter "J" for instance. Think of a person in your family or in your childhood with a "J" in their name who you were very fond of or even loved. Ponder that loving emotion. Think of the happy times you had with this person. Bless that person in your mind. Consider the ability to transfer this feeling to another person in your current life.

Two:, think of a color, for example, blue. Think of something blue that you owned that gave you happiness in the past. Harvest that emotion. Feel it. Try and re-live the joy of having the thing.

Three: Consider one of the five senses (tasting, touching, smelling, hearing, seeing). Select one, such as smell. Remember your favorite aroma. Think back about the flavor or pleasant smell. Ponder the joys of enjoying that aroma again, for example, a great cup of espresso in Venice, Italy. Experience the moments in the past that you enjoyed in conjunction with the feeling and senses. Allow gratitude to fill the mind, Spirit, and body.

Four: Consider the following several methods to achieve the harmonious relationship with your world to be in tune with spiritual abundance:

- Start blessing and praising what is yours.
- Harvest a thankful heart and mind for all of your good fortune such as the ability to do simple things such as think, taste, smell, hear, see, and do, and more.
- Get into nature and wilderness to be still and feel the presence.
- Take a moment to sit or kneel and make a prayer of thanksgiving.
- Write out a list of things that you are thankful for and keep them in your wallet to read whenever you need to refocus on how you are truly blessed and protected by the Universe.
- Quit complaining and begin praising or complimenting others.
- Complement or praise somebody or a family member.
- Think of a person who was truly kind to you.
- Try and remember a person who you think really loves you.
- Think of all those who love or care for you now.

- ➢ Do something for another person to help him or her, or simply write the person a letter or give him or her a flower.
- ➢ Spend time with a spouse, loved one, or child and focus only on wonderful, beautiful, encouraging thoughts about this person.

- **Copyright Image Walter I Anderson – Mentz Private Collection**

Five: See Yourself in Your Mind's Eye

- ➢ See yourself doing what you want to do. Imagine a labor of love.
- ➢ See yourself living where you want to live.
- ➢ See yourself fulfilled in your relationships
- ➢ Act, feel, and think as if you are whom you want to be. This will assist in the growth and enhancement of your total character in reaching Spiritual abundance.

Imagine yourself in the occupation of your dreams. What would it be like? How would you feel? Harvest the emotion of having all you desire. The mind's eye is the picture screen of creation. The more clearly and powerfully you project your images in and onto your consciousness and then to your subconscious, the more easy it will be for your ideals and goals to manifest. As a secret teaching, I would imagine exactly what you want with specificity. Imagine successfully earning the best outcome. Then, I would project that image and feeling into the world, like sending out a letter. Imagine the exact completed successful outcome. You are finished and you can do this exercise later or each day until you have achieved your desire.

Perception and Awareness Exercise

1. Sit is a relaxed position
2. Relax each part of the body and take a few deep breaths.
3. Imagine a warm energy radiating through your body.
4. Enter what we call the Alpha State – which is Relaxed Daydreaming and Right Brain.
5. Now, begin to feel or sense each part of the body.
6. Direct your attention to your toes or hands or ears.
7. Notice how each part of the body feels.
8. Now close your eyes and notice any sounds either of your body or around you.
9. See if you can hear something far away.
10. Now, refocus and imagine just one sound or image.
11. Focus all of your thought on seeing, hearing, feeling, or tasting/smelling only one thing that you imagine.
12. Imagine this one thing to the exclusion of everything else.
13. As an example, try to imagine just the sound of a soft trumpet or French horn playing a song.
14. After a few minutes, relax again and come back to your BETA state of mind and consciousness. Left Brain

Affirmations and Exercises

1. Affirmations are meant to be in the affirmative. Each affirmation can be written in an "AS IF" phrase or sentence in the present tense using the "I Am or I Will" if possible. There is no need to use the "I am Not" style because negative reinforcement is not as effective as Positive Reinforcment".

2. Affirmations can be for health, success, peace, safety, relationships, or even supply in the form of money.

3. Affirmations can be said out loud or in silence. Some people love to do their affirmations in the mirror.

4. A prime example of an affirmation could be, " I am healthy, happy, successfully, loved and whole. I am part of the Supreme Intelligence and the Supreme only creates beauty and perfection."

5. Keep in mind, you should have the idea of the "essence in back of affirmations". As an example, a supply affirmation could say, "I will earn an extra 5000 dollars in the next 4 weeks by providing excellent service as a salesperson or expert or by effectively serving others...." Money is the object but the service and becoming excellence is the essence in back of the object or goal.

6. As you can see, the above affirmation specifies some distinct creative work and cooperation related to your prosperity, and it is not a blind or hopeful demand to receive something for nothing. You can always affirm mentally or out loud for possibilities and opportunities.

7. There are primary reasons against blind affirmations for things or money of which we will not discuss at length. However, if a person demands 100 thousand dollars from the supreme, it may come in the form of an injury settlement which might not be your first choice.

8. Overall, we should state our affirmations with confidence, love, harmony, gratitude, and faith. With this combination, the universe will gladly begin working to unfold opportunities and blessings for you.

9. As such, a clear thought or idea that is repeated again and again is almost certain to manifest a replica of itself

in the future. If the thought is held strongly, with gratitude and feeling, and in a creative way that does not hurt others, your desire will come quickly as the imagined formulation or something even better will unfold.

Spiritual Exercises with Magical Power

1. Basic Prayers for Memory

The first practice is basic prayers. An example of a basic prayer might be the Serenity Prayer by Reinhold Niebuhr: "God grant me the serenity to accept the things I cannot change, the courage to change the things I can, and the wisdom to know the difference." Many other prayers are perfectly acceptable for all types of spiritual seekers. Many of us use the Sermon on the Mount, which includes the Lord's Prayer or "Our Father".

2. Fellowship Exercise

The next activity is seeking wise counsel and fellowship. One of the top types of spiritual practice in the 21st century (also in the 20th century) is seeking out other spiritually minded people who want to grow and heal in a spiritual way. There are two parts to this—you are giving of yourself and you are letting others give to you. For instance, you may be going to a spiritual gathering where you could discuss wisdom literature, the Bible, or some other spiritual literature and sharing your experience about it, sharing your interpretation of it, sharing your strength and hope regarding the discussion or mentoring or counseling or coaching or sponsoring other people. The reward to this is you are giving it away, but you are also teaching it. You are teaching about something even as you are learning about something. Therefore, you are giving it away to keep it. If you give of yourself, invariably, you are receiving the rewards of the universe by trying to help other people who are deeply in need.

3. Active Meditation

Active meditation involves reading certain meditative literature, absorbing what it means, musing over the literature, thinking about it, and discussing it with other people out loud. Sometimes when you have an active meditation for reading it could be something written like a psalm or a proverb or a Bible passage. You may even have a dictionary available to interpret each word amongst other people, and then you discuss it out loud, but you can read it out loud as well before discussing it. To give you an example, some people may be sitting on a train, maybe reading an article in the newspaper and they put the newspaper down and think about it for several minutes and just allow their body to absorb the information and muse over it and then discuss it later. That's an example of active meditation. And a lot of people think they don't have the ability to meditate, but really most people do because if you just show up somewhere for a spiritual discussion you are in the process of actively meditating over something with other people.

4. Seeking Inspiration

The next section is praying for inspiration as a practice. That is when you can either sit down by yourself and get into a relaxed state and ask the universe for ideas or answers, for God's will, for the ability and the strength to do the right thing, and that's what we mean by praying for inspiration or seeking inspiration. One of the truths about inspiration is, you don't have to act on it; you can seek wise counsel about the inspiration that you've received and ask if it's a good idea. Or, you can just run it through a generalized litmus test. Is the idea or is the inspiration something that will help other people, or something that will be unselfish and loving and good for your heart and your mind? Those are things to ask yourself when you seek inspiration and when you decide to act on the inspiration.

5. Seeking God Consciousness

The next section is praying for the presence of the universe and praying for the presence of God. This includes praying for the energy of God and the spirit of the universe to be with you, to be conscious of it, and to cultivate a God-consciousness. Next, you can seek to develop a harmonious relationship with your universe and with your God and to be at peace with yourself, other people, and with nature. Ultimately, if you can ask for all these things and be open to perceiving them, you will actually find that you have developed a consciousness of love of yourself and the world around you. That is the ultimate goal of most orthodox practitioners of spirituality, and that goal is unity and non-separateness, a unity with your authentic self and unity with God and the world.

6. Mass as a Sacrament

Is worship a sacrament. What people overlook is many orthodox spiritual practitioners carry out the ritual of attending a temple or a church or a cathedral or some spiritual house. For the people who attend those services and rituals, those activities are a sacrament, a sacred act. Included in many rituals are singing, chanting, and praying, supplicating, and even circumambulating— a word I like to use that means "walking around." It also refers to the ritual movement of people, whether it be a priest, a rabbi, or other religious leader—the movement of people in a sacred space, asking for and invoking the power and presence of the supernatural into that place of worship—that is a sacrament. The circumambulation, the movement, is certainly a part of the spiritual practice, participating in it, being part of it, and seeing it. Many people actually participate in it by either singing or being part of a choir or being part of the group on the altar that does certain things, and they don't have to be priests, they can just be helping out. So, that is actually a very high orthodox practice.

7. Absorption Exercise:

The first principle is called absorption and it is about how in Mother Nature plants and animals absorb what is around them. They are able to take in the nutrients, food, and sunlight that they need to grow and to be healthy. As human beings and spiritual beings, one of our primary jobs is to learn to absorb the beneficence of the universe, to absorb what is good around us. That includes the sunlight and the trees and the fresh air and the wonderful scents and aromas that we smell in our environment and the sounds and the noises and the animals and the wildlife and the mountains and the beaches to see it, to feel it, to absorb it, to take it in. This is about learning how to pause and take a deep breath and really draw in life's energy, draw in life's energy. The flip side of that is we need to be able to learn to strategically avoid things that rob us of our energy or steal from us without our permission. I know that's not always possible, but we can strategically avoid toxic situations, toxic people, and toxic encounters and avoid escalating situations where the problem can only get worse. Remember that nine out of ten times great miracles can happen when we just walk away and keep our mouth shut, and there is a time and a place for all of us to stand up for ourselves with or against other situations, issues, or people. But in general, and we need to know, you know, when you are in the presence of another person close your eyes and test how you feel around that other person. Are they taking energy from you? Is there a kindred spirit? Do they help you grow? Do they support you? Do they sustain you? This is not only people, but it can be places and things as well.

With this law of absorption you may need to take a few minutes each morning or each evening before you go to bed, close your eyes and take a few deep breaths and relax each part of the body, and then just consciously think to yourself of what is good in the universe, what good happened to you during the day, what blessings happened. Take some time to think about those people who have been good to you over your lifetime and try and feel that goodwill that came to you, feel that love that someone gave to you in the past. It could be your spouse or your aunt or your uncle, your mother, your father or your brother, your sister, or a teacher. Just think of that one person who gave you love and try to be thankful for that in your heart and in your mind. And remember that each day that supply surrounds us, abundance surrounds us—the air, the water, the life. But we must be open in our heart and in our mind to receiving freely of this supply.

8. **Willingness Exercise:**

What kind of willingness is good and healthy? What kind of willpower is good and healthy? The short answer is that when you decide and allow yourself to do something and you take that first step of action, you become willing by moving in the direction of your ideas and your dreams. But the real tough part of it is that you have to learn to exert your will. In doing so, you draw yourself closer to the abundance of the universe and closer to your GOD. , To be willing you have to be able to persist. You have to believe and accept that your goal is possible. Many writers have said the idea wouldn't even be in your mind if it wasn't possible. For many of us it's just difficult to accept and take life's abundance and reach our hands out and let the gift be put in our hands. One famous author used to begin his presentations by holding up $100 bill and saying, "Who wants $100?" It could be a crowd of 1,000 people and finally after 10 or 20 seconds usually one person would finally jump out of their chair and run up there and grab the money. That's the way we have to look at life and sometimes we have to just get up and make our move and take what life is offering us and meet life halfway. Meet Mother Nature halfway. Meet your god and your maker and your creator halfway. Meet the spirit of the universe halfway.

9. **Give it Away Exercise:**

This next little idea is we have to give it to keep it and to learn it to be able to teach it and to be able to tithe in divine ways. We have to be able to give of ourselves the best of ourselves to the universe and the universe will continue to give to us. It doesn't mean you have to donate all your time to charity or donate all of your money to charity, but it does mean that when you are helping others with your spare time or doing the best to support your family and your children, it has a ripple effect on your life and humanity in general. You know, the better you learn to take care of yourself the better you can take care of others. If you learn to take care of your family, you know society will help take care of you.

10.   Character Building Ritual

The thing we have to remember is that our character is what creates our vibration, and our vibration is what attracts things to our life. We have to continue to build our character and that means adding things to our lives that are good for us on a body, mind, and spirit level. And we have to improve those things, while letting go of the things that hold us back and keep us down. This means letting go of the bad habits that keep us from heading in the direction of our dreams. So, our character attracts the same type of energy to us just like two tuning forks vibrate at the same level. It's a type of resonance. It's how we radiate our good feelings. If we radiate vibrations of excellence and advancement and improvement, people will be attracted to us. When people sense we are giving more to life than we are taking from it, the want to do business with us or even have relationships with us.

Sometimes I counsel people whose lives are in a rut and they are trying to make some big changes are stuck, and I always tell them to be careful about getting into a relationship at this time. You have a better chance of making life changes if you are not trying to develop a new relationship, and likewise, you will be available for a meaningful relationship once you get your inner house in order. A person who is going to the gym, taking care of their body and going to school, taking care of their mind, or taking on a new job and getting new skills, will become more attractive to other people.

The next thought is just about your purpose. All of us have to find meaning in life, and we have to pick a purpose. We have to dedicate ourselves to something and choose the direction we want to go in. This could be choosing big goals or a five- or ten-year goal, or it could just be a one-day goal. In any event, you have to pick something. You have to commit to different activities. We have to commit to different tasks and goals and we have to find our purpose. Purpose for us is what you above all want to accomplish, either today or for the rest of your life. Maybe you can't figure that out right now, but at least write it down this question: "What do I really, really want to do, dedicate myself to?" Maybe it could be some niche idea or topic of study or research, just what do I want to specialize in, or what do I want to be the best at? Once you find that goal and you are ready to go forward and never look back— that's usually what defines greatness. People who can pick something and stay focused on it can become great in that particular area if they are willing to commit to it and dedicate their lives to it and never look back.

11.   **Awareness Exercise:**

This next paragraph is about awareness, and for us to be aware we need to wake up. We need to wake up in our minds. We need to see truth regardless of appearances and we need to lose our sense of separateness from the world and allow ourselves to be part of it and to see it, to feel it, to interact with it and be more and more aware of our surroundings. When we do this, we can become saturated with the idea that there is abundance and prosperity in this world.

12.   Association Exercise:

The law of association is about the principle that the energy that
you associate with are what you will become. The more time you
spend with somebody or the more you are in a certain type of
environment, the more one you are going to become one with it and
the more you are going to identify with a certain group of people, a
certain place, or certain types of things.

13.   Creativity:

The next section is creativity. All of us are born with a certain
creativity, a certain type of expression. We have to learn to express
ourselves and express that God-given talent and learn to express it
at the highest level we can. It could be little ideas, it could be little
bits of creativity, it could be making little pieces of art, writing little
poems, creating special clothing, or making little arts and crafts
that people want. Every one of us have our own desires to express
ourselves and be our authentic selves and express our authentic
purpose. What I'm trying to say to you is that unless we head in
the direction of our creativity and use our hands and our minds
and our bodies we may become frustrated in life that we are not
participating in our ideas and our creativeness that belongs to us.

14.   Spiritual Gymnasium

The next thing is about mental and spiritual strength, and I do
believe many of us need to continue in the spiritual gymnasium
everyday to continue in that prosperity and abundance workout
every day. If you can cultivate a prosperity consciousness that
becomes so strong that you are easily able to harvest abundance,
then you will have developed real spiritual strength. You have to
learn to be so strong as to deny and refute the endless possibilities
of something not going your way because it's very easy for us to sit
around and say, oh, this is going to happen, this bad is going to
happen, or this is not going to go my way. It's so easy to be a nega-
holic. But by the same token, if you can focus your mind at
looking at all of the possibilities of greatness and wealth and

abundance and creativity, then you will be immune from the sickness of negativity.

15.   Sacred Days

The next section is about the sacred days, which could include various holidays: Christmas or Easter, St. Joseph's Day, All Saints/Red Mass, 12th Night, or even May Day. Many of these sacred days are based on the lives of Saints, the lives of the masters or, of course, seasonal festivities. Participation in these festivities may call for different rituals, different types of altars, different types of songs, different types of vestments and attire. Some even have a Festival of Saints, for instance, Semana Santa. People in Spain dress up in special outfits and carry large candles and they have different marching groups, and they go through the town. In some of these cities and towns, whether it be Germany or Austria or Span, have these sacred festivals. Some of them are hundreds of years old. They're even in different parts of Germany. They have carnival days which some people call Drei Tolle Tage or Three Crazy Days that goes back almost 800 years as it relates to Carnival Karneval. These are sacred days. These festivities allow people to fellowship and congregate and celebrate certain times of the year. Some people even were able to unwind and relax as a by-product of these festivities. And other types of festivities allow them to enter sacred meditation, sacred prayer, sacred communion with either a spiritual master or holy person like the Mother Mary.

16.   Services and Sacred Space

Another type of ritual is praying the stations of the cross, fasting, or even communion itself. In any of these cases, you may be invoking the Spirit of the Universe, God, or Christ, Mother Mary, or some other master and invoking the presence of that master into your life. And you may also engage in certain types of fasting or dietary restrictions as a symbol of sincerity. With communion and during masses and liturgies, the priests are invoking the presence and the actual energy of God into the alter and congregation, and they're administering that sacred energy or communion to individuals to help unite them with the Holy Spirit as well as remove their sins and help protect them from wickedness.

17.   Nature Bound and Pilgrimages and Commitments

The next type of ritual is a retreat or a time-out or a visit with nature, or even a committed rehabilitation of some sort. There are people who actually take vows with a certain organization perhaps as a monk or an oblate. These are different types of specialized higher rituals with higher degrees of commitment. I've know many families who go on annual retreats together. Some of them are quiet retreats. Some of them are active retreats where they're at a place and eating with others. This type of communal activity is a way to get quiet and relax and get back to the roots of your faith and your life and help draw closer to God and nature. Another example might be a pilgrimage of some sort, such as a hadj or people in Europe that are traveling to a holy place. Some people go to holy places of healing and ask for healing, whether it be in France or Germany or Jerusalem or wherever. In Japan there's these holy places that people go to so they can seek out the energy. Some people refer to these holy places as energy centers. If you've ever been to the top of a pyramid, say in Central America, and felt the energy of that, you would know exactly what I'm talking about. An example of that would be the pyramid in Tepotzlan, Mexico where you can crawl to the top of the mountain. It's a fantastic little way to commune with nature and the heavens. There's actually steps that go up to the top of that mountain.

18.   Retreats

Now another facet of a retreat would be an individual type of retreat. If you look at the old Celtic, Viking, and Norse literature, there were people there that would go sitting. They would do what is called sitting out and commune with themselves. They invoke the presence of nature and they would seek out the inspiration and

guidance of the Fetch, which would be the animal part of their
soul. Some people relate most to a lion or a bear or an eagle. You
can go out into nature and commune with whatever animal part of
your nature that you feel closest to.   It's different than the clan
part of your soul that they call the Sippe. The Fetch, the part of
your animalistic part of your soul, is what some people also
consider your guardian angel. Many people consider that they
have a guardian angel. In some other cultures, that guardian is
believed to be an actual animal itself or that animal part of your
soul, which is fascinating. Some people refer to that in mystical
books as the elemental body.

So, these are various types of things you can do to commune with
yourself and nature and God: retreats, rehabilitation and sitting
out, pilgrimages, and taking in nature, or a nature trip. All of
these are ways to get closer to God and to yourself and to Earth.

19.   Catharsis and Purification

Around the world, regardless of culture and spirituality or tribe,
there are groups that form different purification rituals. These
rituals could be done when a baby is born or comes of age to be
baptized. Purification could be done through either water or
submersion into water, or it could be done through the application
of an ointment **** or smoke. If you've ever seen Native Americans,
sometimes they can smudge a person or blow smoke on them to
purify them and their body or purify a room. That's just an
example of clearing. In the Celtic and Viking literature you'll see
different types of magical clearing of space where they perform
clearing of an area. They could clear to the north and the south
and the east and the west. The geographical points, of course,
were in the upper and the lower, you'll see that in ****, Native
American seven-direction type exercise. So the purification is good
from culture to culture to culture.

What I find interesting is that in the ancient world, including India, purification involves two things, and all catharsis and cleansing and emptying, but in the ancient literature it also included a filling and I think filling is one of the most overlooked aspects of spiritual catharsis and cleansing and purification. Let's say you've been through a tough life and you've had some fears and resentments and some angers and some ideas related to the past that you want to let go; there are two ways to do it. You can try to empty yourself and let go of those issues, those ideas and thoughts, but you can also start filling your mind and your heart with new ideas, new affirmations, new decrees, new empowerments, and new ways of thinking. That also leads to new habits and new actions. Our character is about the totality of our thinking and action and omissions, three different areas; but if you are able to develop new thinking and new habits, you can affect your character. So, developing new ideas, forming new beliefs, and forming new habits, that's really a process of magic that changes us at the core of our being. It changes our DNA structure and it changes our neural pathways, all of that is augmented and changed. And even our future is changed as a by-product of it because if you can continue to clear yourself and add only what's good for you and healthy for you into your life, it affects your life moment to moment and into the future as well. Because if you continue to do good things in the moment then many times it has a ripple effect into the future and with what you think each day in the way you wake up each morning.

20.   Contemplative Action

The next spiritual practice is to become contemplative in action. That means to become mindful of the universe while you are engaging in life's activities, not only mindful but connected to the energy of the universe. Connected to the positive source, which most people call God, so you're connected and contemplative while in action. You're mindful while you're working, and you're connected to that perfect energy. One of the keys to being mindful is to be more aware while you are connected.

So, you're trying to do the right thing, while also being more aware of your surroundings at any given moment, more aware of what's going on inside you. More aware of what's going on outside of you. With that higher awareness, with that higher connection, you're operating at a higher level, and you're not missing out on the signs and symbols and miracles of life, and the gifts that come to you and the people that are sent to you. All of that is extremely important when remaining contemplative in action. It's like being in a meditative state while being active at the same time.

21.   Daily Meditations and Daily Prayers

The next section is about daily liturgy and morning and evening prayers and seasonal prayers. Regardless of what faith and spirituality you are there's probably some good books that can help you in developing your daily meditations, your daily prayers, your daily devotions. All of this is there to help you get into the alpha state, get into the meditative state each day, and become connected to your world and become at peace with yourself and other people. Take a few deep breaths and really prepare for your day, and take time in the evening to prepare to go to sleep, and see if you can be a better person in the next day.

Now, daily liturgy can also mean just a book that you read and meditate over when you're doing your daily prayers. Many people also attend a daily service or an evening or morning mass they could go to with a few people, and that way they're able to pray and commune with each other. They have a little service where they're

able to ask for help, and ask for forgiveness, and for empowerment
to be of service to the world and to their family.

22.   Meditative Objects

The next section is about icons and prayers cards and meditative
objects and services. This is very interesting. I don't know if
you've ever walked in on a maze, a spiritual maze, and taken the
steps according to the actual little walk and made the prayers in
each little section of the maze, but that's just an example of a
prayer type of activity related to yourself, and to the given place.
The other thing is with icons, you may have little icons on your
desk or in your home that remind you of a spiritual master or a
god or a holy mother or Buddha or whatever it might be. The point
of that is just to recognize and be able to have that consciousness
or higher power.

Prayer cards are something smaller. Of course, you can keep them
in your wallet or in your purse and they may have a beautiful
picture on one side and a prayer on the other side. And it's
something you can hold and physically look at and pray. If there's
a special prayer on one side for protection or whatever, it could be
a saint on the card, or it could be Jesus Christ, it could be
Lakshmi, the goddess of progeny and abundance from India, it
doesn't matter. The point being is that it's a physical object that
allows you to stay connected. You're not worshipping the object.
You're just using it as a reminder and a mental refresher of your
commitment to being spiritually connected. In addition, there are
services that are less liturgy oriented, and they're more meditative
oriented. If you've ever been to a Taize service, you'll understand
that it's a type of meditative service in a regular Christian Church
where you try and meditate on an object and an idea in quietude.

23.   Spiritual Jewelry and Charms

Another type of personal ritual and practice that many people have is just the collection of spiritual things to wear whether it be a necklace or a bracelet, or something to hold in your pocket or a keychain, or it could be anything like that or some type of medallion. **** I'm sure some people may even use an earring or some other type of ring, but that's beside the point. I'm not really talking so much about charms and amulets. I'm mainly talking about reminders, reminders of protection and the power of protection, and the power of blessings that you may want to carry with you or wear on your body.

An example would be the cross of St. Benedict. It's a fantastic cross, and it has the Latin words inscribed up and down the cross that a lot of people don't know, but it says "The cross will protect me that goes before me" on one side of it, and on the other side of the cross it says that "No demon will be able to get me." So, it's kind of a fantastic little charm that goes back probably 300 or more years which is really amazing in one particular faith. And that's just one example of a type of charm or a cross that is carried by certain people.

24.   Energy Centers

The next section is about holy places or sacred places, for example a temple, a Hindu temple, or a mosque in a foreign country. For instance, I remember once going to a large mosque, a citadel in Cairo, and going in there to pray, and it's just a fantastic experience and same with a Hindu temple. I've done the same in Singapore. It doesn't matter where you are around the world. In Latin America, I remember going to say some prayers on the top of a Mayan Temple or an Aztec Temple. I later found that this Temple was known for its local warrior god of which many people still pray toward today. So, these are just examples of sacred places that many people have called energy centers around the world that you may want to visit.

25.   Higher Self Visitation Exercises

This idea revolves around cultivating a relationship with your higher self, and one of the exercises and rituals that I've seen is to commune with yourself in a visual way. You would do a visualization or an enhanced meditation where you see yourself meeting with your higher self in a sacred place to commune.

Communing with yourself is a doppelganger type of exercise, because you're meeting with your higher self. To begin this exercise requires your relaxed imagination.   Some people may see themselves as a bird or a falcon flying through the sky, through the forest and landing at the sacred place. Then they morph back into their bodies or into a human being who then walks to the sacred door. Upon opening the door they walk into a great hall and see this other self of theirs up on a throne or maybe at the end of a table, and they sit down and talk to that other self. That other self can look like yourself or it can look like another race; it can have long dark hair, long blonde hair, it can have a crown, or it can be a man or a woman, it doesn't matter. It's what you feel your higher self or higher source would look like. It's part of your soul.

You ask that person questions, deep questions, questions you want to answer, maybe advice, and it may give you something deeper and more authentic than even your own wisdom. It may be able to give you calmer and more sincere answers to questions that you are seeking to answer. The answers may even be different or modified in some way than the ones that you've already come up with by yourself. So, it's a fantastic exercise. Or you could just go there to be thankful, and to be safe with this person, and to commune with this other side of yourself, this higher side that is tapped into the source of all energy.

26.   Mantras

The next section is about prayers and mantras. Sometimes it can be a perfectly good prayer that you've either written by yourself or someone else has written, like the serenity prayer by Reinhold Niebuhr, which is quite famous, or the St. Joseph prayer or any other great prayer. People may use it as a mantra, or just a short prayer that you just may use one word, like God or prosperity or whatever, and you can say this again and again to yourself, silently in meditation or during the course of your day and that's an example of a prayer mantra that you may have.

27.   Prayer for Others and Forgiveness

The next section is praying for others, which is extremely important, and that includes forgiveness. Many people pray for the welfare of their loved ones or family, their children, their relatives, and so forth, and then there's other types of prayers. You may want to pray for somebody who is a leader or pray for someone you dislike or pray for someone that you want to forgive, whether they're living or not living. People who have gone into group therapy or private therapy may at times send a letter to someone or leave a letter on someone's tomb or even facilitate a rite of penitence.

28.   Hospitality Exercise

Another type of spiritual practice or ritual would be just hospitality and this goes back really to the ancient peoples of many cultures, whether it's an Eskimo culture or a German culture or a Russian culture. I'm just giving you some examples. When a stranger comes to your door and they're hungry, that type of hospitality, feeding the individual, the traveler, with food and drink and hospitality and maybe even a place to sleep, all of these things are important. I think maybe today hospitality has been transformed into helping making sure people have a safe place to stay and some healthy food to eat when they're in need. It's very, very important. In its highest form, hospitality honors those who are contributing to humanity and you give or tithe to others to support their good works.

29.   Celtic Action

The next type of ritual would be more of a Celtic prayer ritual. Many Celtic prayers are based in action and activities. There are examples of people who say little prayers along with their actions. They may say a prayer when they do the harvest or a prayer when they serve dinner or a prayer when they kill a beast that will be used to feed the family or the tribe. I'm giving you some shamanic examples, but these are just examples of how specialized prayers are used for everyday activities and everyday events.

30.   Sabbath

The next section is about the Sabbath, having a sacred day during the week, which is about the Sabbath. It could be on Sunday, but in other cultures it may be Friday or a Saturday or another day. Whenever it is, it's having quality time to either take care of yourself or take care of your family members or your children or to commune with nature or to be silent or even in some cultures to commune with your ancestors or those that have gone before you. These are all examples of how the Sabbath is important. Many people attend mass or a church service or a temple or other type of service. So all of this is part of keeping one day special where you can rest and recuperate and be prepared for the rest of your week.

31.   Environmental Exercise

The next section is about an eco-ritual or environmental harmony that's based on many Shamanic cultures, but particularly some of the pagan cultures of ancient Europe and Asia and in Africa. It involves having environment respect and respect for animals, much like the Native Americans did, and respecting the trees and the plants and the crops and even like I had read a book by **** once and he even talked about it. He's a famous Buddhist and he even talked about how he ate his meals he would sometimes pray while eating or pray before or after eating, pray in thankfulness to all the animals and the trees that worked in harmony to create his food. So, all of us want to keep nature unpolluted and protect our forests and our rivers and our mountains, and environmental respect goes back and is a timeless part of spirituality and respect from the beginnings of time until now in many cultures. Trees and other things have been used, either before Christ or afterwards, in the use of sacraments or rituals.

32.   Character Exercise

The next section is about precepts or character building and this is about a ritual. Whether you look at Marcus Aurelius or Ben Franklin, or at the present moment people like Steven Covey, you're looking at your daily activities and how you can be a better person each day and maybe you might make a list at the end of the day of the things you did well and the things you didn't do well and see if you can improve on them. In 12-step lingo, the 10th step focuses on being a good person each day and trying to be good to others and make amends to others when you can. Even if you read the writings of Pythagoras or Buddha you would see this same type of character building virtues in their practices, and with Socrates as well, in virtues and ethics in their daily lives.

33.   Tithe Exercise

Giving and receiving is part of our world. Generosity and giving are timeless activities based on love and compassion. There are 2 types of giving. 1) giving to those who need help 2) giving to those who are expanding their talents, abilities, and craft. Either type of giving is inherently good. Practice giving your time or money to that which inspires you divinely.

Appendix - A Concise Chronology of Esoteric Spirituality

Here is a basic timetable of Esoteric Spirituality and Gnosticism

1. Zarathustra 1000-1500 BC Persia
2. Heraclitus – 6th Century BC
3. Pythagoras – Born 571 BC Century BC Greece – Italy
4. Laozi – Lao Tzu – Taoism Born 571 BC
5. Confucius Born 551 BC
6. Siddhartha Gautama (Buddhism) – 6th Century BC India
7. Socrates, Plato, Aristotle - 4th Century BC
8. Epicurus – 3rd Century BC
9. Cicero 40 BC
10.   Marcus Aurelius 180 AD
11.   Iamblichus 300 AD
12.   St. Benedict 5th Century
13.   Scottus Johannes Erigena – 9th Century
14.   Hildegard von Bingen – 11th Century
15.   Meister Eckhart 13th Century Mystic
16.   Hus – Jacob Boheme – Moravian Piety
17.   Rosicrucians – 14th Century
18.   Martin Luther – 16th Century
19.   Baruch Spinoza - 1632 – 1677
20.   von Zinzendorf und Pottendorf

21.   Liebniz 1710

22.   Hegel 1807

23.   Schopenhauer 1818

24.   Emerson and Thoreau 1860s – American Transcendentalism

25.   Theosophical Groups 1875 to present.

26.   Judge Thomas Troward 1900

27.   Carl Jung – Gnostic Mysticism

28.   Dr. Samuel M Shoemaker – Oxford Movement 1900-1940s

29.   Heȟáka Sápa, commonly known as Black Elk 1863-1950

30.   12 Step Programs – 1930s

31.   21st Century – Wayne Dyer – Eckhart Tolle – The Secret Speakers

Many more people could be included in this chronology as this is a short and generalized list.

Appendix B – Quotes by Famous Physicists and Scientists on Spirituality

- "I am very astonished that the scientific picture of the real world around me is very deficient. It gives a lot of factual information, puts all our experiences in a magnificently consistent order, but is ghastly silent about all and sundry that is really near to our heart, that really matters to us. It cannot tell us a word about red and blue, bitter and sweet, physical pain and physical delight; it knows nothing of beautiful and ugly, good or bad, God and eternity." Erwin Schroedinger (1887-1961)

- "I find it as difficult to understand a scientist who does not acknowledge the presence of a superior rationality behind the existence of the universe as it is to comprehend a theologian who would deny the advances of science." Wernher Von Braun (1912-1977) --German-American rocket scientist

- "Science can have a purifying effect on religion, freeing it from beliefs of a pre-scientific age and helping us to a truer conception of God. At the same time, I am far from believing that science will ever give us the answers to all our questions." Nevill Mott (1905-1996) --English physicist, awarded Nobel Prize in 1977

- "The gift of mental power comes from God, Divine Being, and if we concentrate our minds on that truth, we become in tune with this great power."–Nikola Tesla Tesla was the winner of: Edison Medal (1916); Elliott Cresson Medal (1894); John Scott Medal (1934)

- "Something which is against natural laws seems to me rather out of the question because it would be a depressive idea about God. It would make God smaller than he must be assumed. When he stated that these laws hold, then they hold, and he wouldn't make exceptions. This is too human an idea. Humans do such things, but not God. Max Born, who was instrumental in the development of quantum mechanics. Nobel Prize winning physicist

- "The first gulp from the glass of natural sciences will turn you into an atheist, but at the bottom of the glass God is waiting for you." –Werner Heisenberg, 1932 Nobel Prize in Physics for the creation of quantum mechanics.

- "…Those laws are within the grasp of the human mind. God wanted us to recognize them by creating us after his own image so that we could share in his own thoughts… and if piety allow us to say so, our understanding is in this respect of the same kind as the divine, at least as far as we are able to grasp something of it in our mortal life." –Johannes Kepler, the German mathematician and astronomer who is considered to be one of the founders of the field of astronomy.

- "Another source of conviction in the existence of God, connected with the reason and not with the feelings, impresses me as having much more weight. This follows from the extreme difficulty or rather impossibility of conceiving this immense and wonderful universe, including man with his capacity of looking far backwards and far into futurity, as the result of blind chance or necessity. When thus reflecting I feel compelled to look to a First Cause having an intelligent mind in some degree analogous to that of man; and I deserve to be called a Theist." –Charles Darwin, the founder of evolutionary biology, as quoted in his autobiography.

- "Whence it follows that God is absolutely perfect, since perfection is nothing but magnitude of positive reality, in the strict sense, setting aside the limits or bounds in things which are limited." –Gottfried Leibniz, the German mathematician and philosopher (1646-1716) who founded calculus.

- "The best data we have (concerning the Big Bang) are exactly what I would have predicted, had I nothing to go on but the five books of Moses, the Psalms, the Bible as a whole." –Arno Penzias, the 1978 Nobel Prize recipient in physics.

- "To know the mighty works of God, to comprehend His wisdom and majesty and power; to appreciate, in degree, the wonderful workings of His laws, surely all this must be a pleasing and acceptable mode of worship to the Most High, to whom ignorance cannot be more grateful than knowledge." –Nicolaus Copernicus, the mathematician and astronomer (1473-1543).

- "Science is a game – but a game with reality, a game with sharpened knives. If a man cuts a picture carefully into 1000 pieces, you solve the puzzle when you reassemble the pieces into a picture; in the success or failure, both your intelligences compete. In the presentation of a scientific problem, the other player is the good Lord. He has not only set the problem but also has devised the rules of the game – but they are not completely known, half of them are left for you to discover or to deduce. The uncertainty is how many of the rules God himself has permanently ordained, and how many apparently are caused by your own mental inertia, while the solution generally becomes possible only through freedom from its limitations. This is perhaps the most exciting thing in the game." –Erwin Schroedinger, winner of the 1933 Nobel Prize in Physics.

- "The atoms or elementary particles themselves are not real; they form a world of potentialities or possibilities rather than one of things or facts." Werner Heisenberg

- "Science is not only compatible with spirituality; it is a profound source of spirituality. When we recognize our place in an immensity of light-years and in the passage of ages, when we grasp the intricacy, beauty, and subtlety of life, then that soaring feeling, that sense of elation and humility combined, is surely spiritual...The notion that science and spirituality are somehow mutually exclusive does a disservice to both." Carl Sagan (1934-1996)

- "Observations not only disturb what is to be measured, they produce it." Pascual Jordan

Quotes on Prosperity and Abundance

- "It is wealth to be content." —Lao-Tzu

- "Wealth is not his that has it, but his who enjoys it." —Benjamin Franklin

- "Life is a field of unlimited possibilities." —Deepak Chopra

- "He who is plenteously provided for from within, needs but little from without." —Johann Wolfgang von Goethe

- "Take full account of the excellencies which you possess, and in gratitude remember how you would hanker after them, if you had them not." —Marcus Aurelius

- "Whenever anything negative happens to you, there is a deep lesson concealed within it, although you may not see it at the time." —Eckhart Tolle

- "If you want to change who you are, begin by changing the size of your dream. Even if you are broke, it does not cost you anything to dream of being rich. Many poor people are poor because they have given up on dreaming." —Robert Kiyosaki

- "Ideas are the beginning points of all fortunes." —Napoleon Hill

- "When you are grateful fear disappears and abundance appears." —Anthony Robbins

- "Everything in the universe has a purpose. Indeed, the invisible intelligence that flows through everything in a purposeful fashion is also flowing through you." —Dr. Wayne Dyer

- "Gratitude is an attitude that hooks us up to our source of supply. And the more grateful you are, the closer you become to your maker, to the architect of the universe, to the spiritual core of your being. It's a phenomenal lesson." —Bob Proctor

- "Living in Abundance and Prosperity is a Reasonable Option" — Magus Incognito

- "You have a divine right to abundance, and if you are anything less than a millionaire, you haven't had your fair share." —Stuart Wilde

- "Prosperity is not just having things. It is the consciousness that attracts the things. Prosperity is a way of living and thinking, and not just having money or things. Poverty is a way of living and thinking, and not just a lack of money or things." —Eric Butterworth

- "Most folks are about as happy as they make up their minds to be." —Abraham Lincoln

- "And he shall be like a tree planted by the rivers of water, that bringeth forth his fruit in his season; his leaf also shall not wither; and whatsoever he doeth shall prosper." (Psalm 1:3)

- "The Constitution only gives people the right to pursue happiness. You have to catch it yourself." —Benjamin Franklin

- *Not what we have But what we enjoy, constitutes our abundance.* ~ *Epicurus*

- "Gratitude is the vital ingredient in the recipe for Faith" —Magus Incognito

- "We may divide thinkers into those who think for themselves and those who think through others. The latter are the rule and the former the exception. The first are original thinkers in a double sense, and egotists in the noblest meaning of the word." —Arthur Schopenhauer

- "The key to every man is his thought. Sturdy and defiant though he look he has a helm which he obeys, which is the idea after which all his facts are classified. He can only be reformed by showing him a new idea which commands his own." —Ralph Waldo Emerson

- "All truly wise thoughts have been thought already thousands of times; but to make them really ours we must think them over again honestly till they take root in our personal expression." — Johann Wolfgang von Goethe.

- "Great men are they who see that spirituality is stronger than any material force; that thoughts rule the world." —Ralph Waldo Emerson.

- "All that we are is a result of what we have thought." —Buddha

- "Wealth is the slave of a wise man. The master of a fool." —Seneca

- "Happiness is not in the mere possession of money; it lies in the joy of achievement, in the thrill of creative effort." —Franklin D Roosevelt

- *Money is like manure. You have to spread it around or it smells. ~ J. Paul Getty*

- "Liberty is not a means to a higher political end. It is the highest political end." - Lord John Dalberg-Acton

- "We are what we repeatedly do. Excellence, then, is not an act but a habit." —Aristotle

- *Money is like love; it kills slowly and painfully the one who withholds it, and enlivens the other who turns it on his fellow man. ~ Kahlil Gibran*

- *Empty pockets never held anyone back. Only empty heads and empty hearts can do that. ~ Norman Vincent Peale*

- "The thief cometh not, but for to steal, and to kill, and to destroy: I am come that they might have life, and that they might have it more abundantly." (John 10:10, KJV)

- Prosperity is not without many fears and distastes, and adversity is not without comforts and hopes. ~Francis Bacon

- "It is health that is real wealth and not pieces of gold and silver." ~ Mahatma Gandhi

- "Desire is the starting point of all achievement, not a hope, not a wish, but a keen pulsating desire, which transcends everything.

When your desires are strong enough you will appear to possess
superhuman powers to achieve."
~ Napoleon Hill

• "Move out of your comfort zone. You can only grow if you are willing
  to feel awkward and uncomfortable when you try something new."
  ~ Brian Tracy

• "You can open your mind to prosperity when you realize the true
  definition of the word: You are prosperous to the degree you are
  experiencing peace, health and plenty in your world."
  ~ Catherine Ponder, Open Your Mind to Prosperity

• There is a science of getting rich and it is an exact science, like
  algebra or arithmetic. There are certain laws which govern the
  process of acquiring riches and once these laws are learned and
  obeyed by anyone, that person will get rich with mathematical
  certainty. ~ Wallace D Wattles

• Within you right now is the power to do things you never dreamed
  possible. This power becomes available to you just as soon as you
  can change your beliefs. ~ Dr Maxwell Maltz

• *"Far better it is to dare mighty things, to win glorious triumphs even
  though checkered by failure, than to rank with those timid spirits
  who neither enjoy nor suffer much because they live in the gray
  twilight that knows neither victory nor defeat."* ~ **Theodore
  Roosevelt -** 26th President of the U.S. and winner of the 1906
  Nobel Peace Prize.

About George Mentz

Commissioner George Mentz is a premier, sought-after speaker, revolutionary author, and global management consultant. Dr. Mentz is universally referenced by his clientele, friends and colleagues, as one of the most thoughtful, enthusiastic, and empathetic leaders in the business world today.   George Mentz, an international lawyer and passionate professor, is the founder of the GAFM Global Academy of Financial Management ® and he has published extensively in the fields of law, e-business, SEO, entrepreneurship, marketing, international finance, and success strategy. George Mentz has advised and consulted with the US Government , United Nations, & Fortune 500 companies on domestic and international strategy while helping people from around the world improve their education and careers.

George Mentz and his companies have held seminars and VIP courses in over 35 countries worldwide. Professor Mentz received his Doctor of Jurisprudence and MBA degrees after attending legal and business coursework at Loyola University, Catholique University Belgium, William and Mary Law School, Tulane University in the USA, Austria, Spain, Mexico and Brazil.   Mentz is the first person in the United States to achieve "Quad Designation" Status as a JD, MBA, qualified/licensed financial planner and wealth manager, and Qualified/Certified Financial Consultant & Planner.   Counselor Mentz is the recipient of national awards and honors for his contributions in the fields of management, excellence, teaching, charity, leadership, and speaking In recent years, George Mentz has been named a expert and leader for his publications and he has been honored by mainstream media as a brain trust member and part of the Dream Team of Financial Writers for mainstream media outlets. George Mentz has served on the advisory boards of: The Global Finance Forum in Switzerland, The World E-Commerce Forum in the UK, The Certified Economist Association of Africa, and the China Wealth Management Institute of Hong Kong, The Arab Academy Standards Council, The International Project Management Commission, a US Medical School, a Law School's Graduate Program, and various charities. Mentz is a syndicated author and 2 time national award winning professor is a contributor and expert for various organizations where some of Dr. Mentz's bestselling books and publications include: CWM Chartered Wealth Manager Guide, Project Manager Executive Guide, Internet College Recruiting and Marketing, The Wealth Management Executive Guide, Online Credibility in the Finance World – Protecting Your Web Reputation & Company Brand, The Secret Powers of Highly Effective People, Spiritual Wealth Management, Wealth Management and Financial Planning, and many more. Published in many journals, Mentz is a pioneer in the movements of: executive certification training, international wealth management, internet marketing and human-potential through neuroplasticity. Mentz and his executive development companies are Accredited by the TUV Austria, ISO Certified for Quality, and have been featured or quoted in the NASDAQ News, Forbes, Reuters, Morningstar, Yahoo Finance, Wall Street Globe, The Hindu National, El Norte Latin America, the Financial Times, NYSSA New York Securities Analysts News, The China Daily, The Department of Education ERIC Library, The US Department of Labor Brochures, Black Enterprise, The San Francisco Chronicle, Associated Press, & The Arab Times. http://www.GeorgeMentz.com   You can contact Dr.jur. G.S. Mentz at his website, www.gmentz.com

Other References or Authors of Interest

1. Allen, J. (1998). *As You Think*. Ed. with introduction by M. Allen. Novato, CA: New World Library
2. Behrend, G. (1927) Your Invisible Power. Montana: Kessinger Publishing.
3. Carnegie, D. (1994). *How to Win Friends and Influence People.* New York: Pocket Books. http://www.dalecarnegie.com
4. Carlson, R. (2001). *Don't Sweat the Small Stuff About Money.* Location: Hyperion. Previously published as *Don't Worry Make Money* http://www.dontsweat.com.
5. Chopra, D. (1996). *The Seven Spiritual Laws of Success.* London: Bantam Press. http://www.chopra.com
6. Collier, R. (1970). *Be Rich.* Oak Harbor, WA: Robert Collier Publishing. http://robertcollierpublications.com
7. Covey, S. R. (1989). *The 7 Habits of Highly Effective People.* London: Simon & Schuster. http://www.stephencovey.com
8. Dyer, W. (1993). *Real Magic: Creating Miracles in Everyday Life.* New York: HarperCollins. http://www.drwaynedyer.com
9. Gawain, Shakti (1979). *Creative Visualization.* Mill Valley: Publisher. http://www.shaktigawain.com
10. Mentz (2006). *How to Master Abundance and Prosperity - The* Master Key System *Decoded.* Location: Mentz Pub.
11. Hill, Napoleon (1960). *Think and Grow Rich,* New York: Fawcett Crest.
12. Hill, Napoleon, W.D. Wattles, R. Collier, et al. (2010) How to Be Rich: Tarcher Penguin http://www.tarcherbooks.net/new-release-how-to-be-rich
13. His Holiness the Dalai Lama & Howard C. Cutler (1999). *The Art of Happiness: A handbook for Living.* London: Hodder & Stoughton. http://www.dalailama.com
14. James, William (1902). *The Varieties of Religious Experience.* Location: Publisher.
15. Maltz, Maxwell, MD. Psycho-Cybernetics. New York. Pocket Books 1960
16. Marden, O. S. (1997). *Pushing to the Front, or Success under Difficulties,* Vols 1 & 2. Santa Fe, CA: Sun Books.

17.   Mentz, G. S. (2006) *Other Books and Summaries on The Secrets of Life and Abundance:* www.gmentz.com or

18.   Mulford, Prentice (1908). *Thoughts are Things - Essays Selected From The White Cross Library.* Location: Publisher.

19.   Murphy, J. (1963). *The Power of Your Subconscious Mind,* New Jersey: Prentice Hall.

20.   Ponder, C. (1962) *The Dynamic Laws of Prosperity,* Camarillo, CA: DeVorss & Co.

21.   Roman & Packer (1988). *Creating Money:* Tiburon, CA: Kramer. http://www.orindaben.com

22.   Price, J. R. (1987). *The Abundance Book.* Carlsbad, CA: Hay House. http://www.johnrandolphprice.com

23.   Smiles, S. (2002). *Self-Help: With Illustrations of Character, Conduct, and Perseverance.* Oxford, UK: Oxford University Press.

24.   Tracy, B. (1993). *Maximum Achievement: Strategies and Skills That Will Unlock Your Hidden Powers to Succeed.* New York: Fireside. http://www.briantracy.com

25.   Troward, Judge Thomas (1904). *The Edinburgh Lectures on Mental Science.* Location: Publisher.

26.   Wattles, W.D. (1976). *Financial Success through the Power of Thought* [*The Science of Getting Rich*]. Rochester, Vermont: Destiny Books. (Written originally around 1910).

Disclaimer

For the sections on Philosophy and Religions, this is a beginner's text and the information about religions and philosophy is in condensed form. A seeker may spend years learning about any one philosophy. Some religions were left out of this book as the author may not know enough about the religion or teachings to make a presentation. This work consists of original works created from analyzing the philosophy of the great teachers of the past, and the creative revision, original insights, revised or updated public domain works, or the enhancement of the philosophy of great thinkers. From the Dark Ages to the Reformation and Enlightenment, the world began to study, interpret, and deliver universal truth, tactics of prosperity, and secrets of obtaining peace of mind. Some are pre-1925 public domain concepts are contained herein along with timeless ideas which cannot be attributed..

All readers are advised to find a licensed professional before making any important medical, legal, health, tax, or financial decision. Always seek the advice of competent counsel or physician with any questions you may have regarding a medical issue. As advice must be tailored to the specific circumstances of each person and case, and laws and advice are constantly changing. No legal, health or medical advice is intended to be given in this book. The advice in this book are generalized suggestions where many have benefited from implementing various ideas herein.

---

[i] W. D. Wattles enhanced by Prof. Mentz from "Financial Success Through Creative Thought " 1910
[ii] W.D. Wattles - How to Be a Genius 1911
[iii] I W. D. Wattles enhanced by Prof. Mentz from "Financial Success Through Creative Thought " 1910
[iv] The Science of Being Great" by Wattles – Elizabeth Towne Publishing 1914

- Excerpts, paragraphs, and selected content in this book are from pre-1925 writings of: Wallace Wattles, Christian Larson, William Walker Atkinson, and Genevieve Behrend

Other References or Authors of Interest

Allen, J. (1998). *As You Think*. Ed. with introduction by M. Allen. Novato, CA: New World Library

Behrend, G. (1927) Your Invisible Power. Montana: Kessinger Publishing.

Carnegie, D. (1994). *How to Win Friends and Influence People*. New York: Pocket Books. http://www.dalecarnegie.com

Carlson, R. (2001). *Don't Sweat the Small Stuff About Money*. Location: Hyperion. Previously published as *Don't Worry Make Money* http://www.dontsweat.com.

Chopra, D. (1996). *The Seven Spiritual Laws of Success*. London: Bantam Press. http://www.chopra.com

Collier, R. (1970). *Be Rich*. Oak Harbor, WA: Robert Collier Publishing. http://robertcollierpublications.com

Covey, S. R. (1989). *The 7 Habits of Highly Effective People*. London: Simon & Schuster. http://www.stephencovey.com

Dyer, W. (1993). *Real Magic: Creating Miracles in Everyday Life*. New York: HarperCollins. http://www.drwaynedyer.com

Gawain, Shakti (1979). *Creative Visualization*. Mill Valley: Publisher. http://www.shaktigawain.com

Haanel, Mentz (2006). *How to Master Abundance and Prosperity - The* Master Key System *Decoded*. Location: Xlibris Pub.

Carlson Haanel Wattles, Mentz (2005). *The Science of Growing Rich*. Location: Xlibris Publishing.

Hill, N. (1960). *Think and Grow Rich*, New York: Fawcett Crest.

His Holiness the Dalai Lama & Howard C. Cutler (1999). *The Art of Happiness: A handbook for Living*. London: Hodder & Stroughton. http://www.dalailama.com

James, William (1902). *The Varieties of Religious Experience*. Location: Publisher.

Maltz, Maxwell, MD. Psycho-Cybernetics. New York. Pocket Books 1960

Marden, O. S. (1997). *Pushing to the Front, or Success under Difficulties*, Vols 1 & 2. Santa Fe, CA: Sun Books.

Mentz, G. S. (2006) *Other Books and Summaries on The Secrets of Life and Abundance:* http://www.lulu.com/gmentz

Mulford, Prentice (1908). *Thoughts are Things - Essays Selected From The White Cross Library.* Location: Publisher.

Murphy, J. (1963). *The Power of Your Subconscious Mind*, New Jersey: Prentice Hall.

Ponder, C. (1962) *The Dynamic Laws of Prosperity*, Camarillo, CA: DeVorss & Co.

Roman & Packer (1988). *Creating Money*: Tiburon, CA: Kramer. http://www.orindaben.com

Price, J. R. (1987). *The Abundance Book*. Carlsbad, CA: Hay House. http://www.johnrandolphprice.com

Smiles, S. (2002). *Self-Help: With Illustrations of Character, Conduct, and Perseverance. Oxford, UK: Oxford University Press.*

Tracy, B. (1993). *Maximum Achievement: Strategies and Skills That Will Unlock Your Hidden Powers to Succeed*. New York: Fireside. http://www.briantracy.com

Troward, Judge Thomas (1904). *The Edinburgh Lectures on Mental Science*. Location: Publisher.

Wattles, W.D. (1976). *Financial Success through the Power of Thought* [*The Science of Getting Rich*]. Rochester, Vermont: Destiny Books. (Written originally around 1910).

Wilkinson, Bruce (2000). *The Prayer of Jabez*. City, OR: Multnamah Publishers. http://www.prayerofjabez.com

This work is mostly original works created from analyzing the philosophy of the great teachers of the past, and the creative revision, original insights, revised or updated public domain works

[v] W.D. Wattles - IBID
[vi] Pagels, Elaine. *The Gnostic Gospels*, Vintage Press, 1989, pgs. 18, 37, 42